Our America and Theirs

Kennedy and the Alliance for Progress—
The Debate at Punta del Este

Che Guevara Publishing Project

These books form part of a series published by Ocean Press and the Che Guevara Studies Center of Havana, with the objective of disseminating the works and ideas of Che Guevara.

Self-Portrait
A Photographic and Literary Memoir

The Motorcycle Diaries
Notes on a Latin American Journey

Another Latin American Journey
A Second Look at the Continent

Reminiscences of the Cuban Revolutionary War
Authorized Edition

The Congo Diary
Reminiscences of the Congolese Revolutionary War

The Bolivian Diary
Authorized Edition

Che Guevara Reader
Writings on Politics and Revolution

Latin America
Awakening of a Continent

Global Justice
Liberation and Socialism

Guerrilla Warfare
Authorized Edition

Our America and Theirs
Kennedy and the Alliance for Progress

The Great Debate on Political Economy
A Humanist Approach to Marxist Economics

Critical Notes On Political Economy
A Critical Analysis of the Soviet Economic System

The Philosophical Notebooks
Writings on Marxism and Revolutionary Humanism

Socialism and Humanity in Cuba
A Classic Edition

Our America and Theirs
Kennedy and the Alliance for Progress—
The Debate at Punta del Este

Ernesto Che Guevara

Edited by María del Carmen Ariet García and Javier Salado

Centro de Estudios
CHE GUEVARA

Ocean Press

Melbourne ▪ New York
www.oceanbooks.com.au

Front and back cover photographs: Che Guevara at the 1961 Punta del Este conference

Cover design by David Spratt

ISBN 10: 1-876175-81-8
ISBN 13: 978-1-876175-81-8
Library of Congress Catalog Card No: 2005937902

First Printed 2006

PUBLISHED BY OCEAN PRESS

Australia: GPO Box 3279, Melbourne, Victoria 3001, Australia
           Fax: (61-3) 9329 5040 Tel: (61-3) 9326 4280
           E-mail: info@oceanbooks.com.au
USA: PO Box 1186, Old Chelsea Stn., New York, NY 10113-1186, USA
           Tel/Fax: (1-212) 260 3690

OCEAN PRESS DISTRIBUTORS

United States and Canada: Consortium Book Sales and Distribution
           Tel: 1-800-283-3572   www.cbsd.com
Australia and New Zealand: Palgrave Macmillan
           E-mail: customer.service@macmillan.com.au
UK and Europe: Turnaround Publisher Services
           E-mail: orders@turnaround-uk.com
Cuba and Latin America: Ocean Press
           E-mail: oceanhav@enet.cu

ocean
www.oceanbooks.com.au
info@oceanbooks.com.au

Contents

Preface

In proposing the Alliance for Progress at a reception for Latin American diplomats at the White House on March 13, 1961, President Kennedy invoked the names of revolutionary heroes of the Americas: Simón Bolivar, José Martí, San Martín, Thomas Jefferson and George Washington. The Alliance for Progress, he said, would "complete the revolution in the Americas" and inaugurate a new era of peace and prosperity for the continent.

The US president remarked to the assembled diplomats, "As a citizen of the United States let me be the first to admit that we North Americans have not always grasped the significance of this common mission."

This "alliance of free governments," said Kennedy, had to commit itself to "eliminate tyranny from a hemisphere in which it has no rightful place." Cuba was specifically singled out and Kennedy expressed the hope that the people of Cuba would "soon rejoin the society of free men," a comment that might have been an oblique reference to the fact that at the very moment President Kennedy delivered this speech, final preparations were being made for the attack on Cuba by a US-trained mercenary army.

The Punta del Este conference in August 1961 took place at one of the lowest points of US-Cuba relations, only a few months after the failed Bay of Pigs invasion. Less than a year into his administration, Cuba had already become almost an obsession for President Kennedy. Immediately following the political and military defeat inflicted by Cuba in April 1961, a new program of covert action was set in motion to undermine and hopefully overthrow the revolutionary government in Havana.

In this regard, the late-night encounter a few months later during the Punta del Este conference between Kennedy's special aide Richard Goodwin and Che Guevara was highly significant. While Goodwin's memo about this meeting to President Kennedy remained a classified document for decades, Che Guevara described it in the televised press conference (see Press Conference on Cuban TV, August 23, 1961, in this book).

Accompanying his memo, Goodwin sent Kennedy an additional note, in which he gave his assessment of the situation and made various proposals. He stated his view that although "Cuba desires an understanding with the US," he nevertheless recommended intensifying military and economic pressure and extending the trade embargo.

He concluded that the "below ground dialogue which Che has begun" should be pursued, but only if Cuba shows it is ready to "sever communist ties and begin democratization. In this way we can begin to probe for the split in the top leadership which might exist."

This should all be done as "quietly" as possible, he suggested, as too much focus on Cuba would "allow them to appear as the victims of US aggression." It was important not to "create the impression we are obsessed with Cuba—an impression which only strengthens Castro's hand in Cuba and encourages anti-American and leftist forces in other countries to rally around the Cuban flag."

Goodwin described in great detail his informal meeting with Che Guevara at a birthday party for a Brazilian delegate in his memo to President Kennedy dated August 22, 1961:

> The conversation took place the evening of August 17 at 2 a.m. Several members of the Brazilian and Argentine delegations had made efforts — throughout the Punta del Este conference — to arrange a meeting between me and Che. This was obviously done with Che's approval, if not his urging. I had avoided such a meeting during the conference...
>
> Che was wearing green fatigues, and his usual overgrown and scraggly beard. Behind the beard his features are quite soft, almost feminine, and his manner is intense. He has a good sense of humor, and there was considerable joking back and forth during the meeting. He seemed very ill at ease when we began to talk, but soon became relaxed and spoke freely. Although he left no doubt of his personal and intense devotion to communism, his conversation was free of propaganda and bombast. He spoke calmly, in a straightforward manner, and with the appearance of detachment and objectivity. He left no doubt, at any time, that he felt completely free to speak for his government and rarely distinguished between his personal observations and the official position of the Cuban government. I had the definite impression that he had thought out his remarks very carefully — they were extremely well organized. I told him at the outset that I had no authority to negotiate my country's problems, but would report what he said to interested officials of our government. He said "good" and began.
>
> Guevara began by saying that I must understand the

Cuban revolution. They intend to build a socialist state, and the revolution which they have begun is irreversible. They are also now out of the US sphere of influence, and that too is irreversible. They will establish a single-party system with Fidel as secretary general of the party. Their ties with the East stem from natural sympathies, and common beliefs in the proper structure of the social order. They feel that they have the support of the masses for their revolution, and that that support will grow as time passes.

He said that the United States must not act on the false assumptions that (a) we can rescue Cuba from the claws of communism (he meant by other than direct military action); (b) that Fidel is a moderate surrounded by a bunch of fanatic and aggressive men, and might be moved to the Western side; (c) that the Cuban revolution can be overthrown from within — there is, he said, diminishing support for such an effort and it will never be strong enough.

He spoke of the great strength of the Cuban revolution, and the impact it has had on liberal thought throughout Latin America. For example, he said, all the leftwing forces in Uruguay were joining forces under the banner of Cuba. He said civil war would break out in many countries if Cuba were in danger — and such war might break out in any event. He spoke with great intensity of the impact of Cuba on the continent and the growing strength of its example.

He said that in building a communist state they had not repeated all of the aggressive moves of the East. They did not intend to construct an iron curtain around Cuba but to welcome technicians and visitors from all countries to come and work.

He touched on the matter of the plane thefts. He said he didn't know if I knew but they had not been responsible for any hijackings. The first plane was taken by a young fellow who was a good boy but a little wild and who is now in jail.

They suspected that the last plane was taken by a provocateur (a CIA agent). He is afraid that if these thefts keep up it will be very dangerous.

He began to discuss the difficulties of the Alliance for Progress. He asked me if I had heard his speech at the closing of the conference. I said I had listened to it closely. He said that it explained his viewpoint on the Alliance for Progress. (In this speech he said the idea of the Alianza was fine, but it would fail. He spoke also of the play of historical forces working on behalf of communism, etc. — that there would be either leftist revolutions or rightist coups leading to leftist takeovers, and there was also a strong chance that the commies would get in through popular election.) He then said he wished to add that there was an intrinsic contradiction in the Alianza — by encouraging the forces of change and the desires of the masses we might set loose forces which were beyond our control, ending in a Cuba style revolution. Never once did he indicate that Cuba might play a more direct role in the march of history.

He then said, now that he had discussed our difficulties he would like to discuss his own problems — and he would like to do so frankly. There were in Cuba, he said, several basic problems:

1. There was disturbing revolutionary sentiment, armed men and sabotage.

2. The small bourgeoisie were hostile to the revolution or, at best were lukewarm.

3. The Catholic Church (here he shook his head in dismay).

4. Their factories looked naturally to the US for resources, especially spare parts and at times the shortages of these resources made things very critical.

They had accelerated the process of development too rapidly and their hard currency reserves were very low. Thus they were unable to import consumer goods and meet basic needs of the people.

He then said that they didn't want an understanding with the United States because they know that was impossible. They would like a *modus vivendi*—at least an interim *modus vivendi*. Of course, he said, it was difficult to put forth a practical formula for such a *modus vivendi*—he knew because he had spent a lot of time thinking about it. He thought we should put forth such a formula because we had public opinion to worry about whereas he could accept anything without worrying about public opinion.

I said nothing, and he waited and then said that, in any event, there were some things he had in mind.

1. That they would not give back the expropriated properties—the factories and banks—but they could pay for them in trade.

2. They could agree not to make any political alliance with the East—although this would not affect their natural sympathies.

3. They would have free elections—but only after a period of institutionalizing the revolution had been completed. In response to my question he said that this included the establishment of a one-party system.

4. Of course, they would not attack Guantánamo. (At this point he laughed as if at the absurdly self-evident nature of such a statement.)

5. He indicated, very obliquely, and with evident reluctance because of the company in which we were talking, that they could also discuss the activities of the Cuban revolution in other countries.

He then went on to say that he wanted to thank us very much for the invasion—that it had been a great political victory for them—enabled them to consolidate—and transformed them from an aggrieved little country to an equal.

Guevara said he knew it was difficult to negotiate these things but we could open up some of these issues by beginning to discuss subordinate issues. He suggested discussion of the airplane issue (presumably, we would use the airplane issue as a cover for more serious conversation).

He said they could discuss no formula that would mean giving up the type of society to which they were dedicated.

At close he said that he would tell no one of the substance of this conversation except Fidel. I said I would not publicize it either.

Within a few months of this conversation, yet another invasion plan was initiated by the CIA and US State Department as part of Operation Mongoose to topple the revolutionary government and assassinate Fidel Castro, a plan that culminated in the Missile Crisis of October 1962.

Ocean Press
2006

Introduction

The publishing of the memoirs of the Punta del Este conference arose as a project of Ocean Press after the Che Guevara Studies Center held a seminar in Havana in August 2001, the main aim of which was to reflect on the relevance and timeliness of the positions taken by the Cuban delegation 40 years before, especially as expressed by Ernesto Che Guevara.

The Inter-American Economic and Social Council (CIES) meeting that took place in August 1961 at Punta del Este, Uruguay, was called to discuss the initiative that US President John F. Kennedy had announced on March 13, 1961, which became known as the Alliance for Progress. Participants in the Punta del Este conference set forth the 10 basic points of the Alliance, whose purpose was to provide the Latin American countries with funds for their development and progress. Employing rhetoric that was rather unusual for the era, the promoters of the Alliance claimed that its points were based on Bolívar's aspiration of making Latin America the greatest region in the world.

Of course, it was clear to everyone familiar with US hemispheric policy that the real purpose for calling the Punta del Este conference was to discuss the presence and existence of the Cuban revolution and to provide another opportunity for the US government to try desperately to overthrow it. We should not forget that the "new" proposals for change were only words, as the fundamental nature of Washington's relations with Latin America remained unaltered. While wielding the "big stick" more discreetly, the United States clearly outlined the implementation of a project that would guarantee its complete economic and political hegemony in the region.

This is the only explanation for the fact that, just a month earlier, in a speech on aid for and cooperation with Latin America, Kennedy had announced the United States would invade the island of Cuba because it feared that Cuba's example and "foreign ideology" were contagious. It was a classic case of perpetuating the Cold War as had been done in many countries on many occasions, ignoring the people's feelings and desire to achieve true independence.

In view of Cuba's ongoing example and pressured by circumstances after the shameful defeat at the Bay of Pigs only a few months before, the United States desperately stepped up preparations for the OAS conference so as to implement the Kennedy plan of aid and collaboration, without bothering to hide that it was essentially designed to guarantee the security of and support for the United States.

In this way, the "good intentions" for outlining the future path that the hemisphere would take—intentions that Douglas Dillon, US treasury secretary, expressed in his address inaugurating the Punta del Este conference—were revoked when the United States resorted to its already worn-out classic approach of the stick and the carrot to convince the Latin American countries that Cuba posed a danger.

The timely and effective speeches Che gave at the 1961 Punta del Este conference are contained in this book. They were constructive, even though, as he stated at the time, he was convinced the proposed measures were simply crumbs and false promises which would have no appreciable results. Che described the political nature of the conference, pointing out its direct relationship to the economy and warning that, in view of the use of precise proposals and grandiloquent statements, the participants should think about the creation of rational plans for development and about real coordination of technical and financial assistance by the industrialized countries, in order to safeguard the interests of the weaker countries and protect their nations against acts of economic aggression by other member countries.

Che and the Cuban delegation smoothed the way for engaging in a harmonious process at Punta del Este, even though they knew what the true intentions and scope of the Alliance were, and they helped prepare the bases of a truly progressive plan that would benefit the many instead of the few. The Cuban team's suggestions, both in the plenary session and in the commissions, remain very timely because of their realistic language and denunciation of the dangers of the proposed economic integration and of the threat the international monopolies constituted due to their stranglehold over trade in the region through the free trade associations.

The Cubans at Punta del Este consistently challenged the US delegation's specious arguments, and the conference conclusions confirmed Che's warning that it had been called to oppose Cuba's example in Latin America and that it would be unable to adopt measures in line with the reality prevailing in our countries. Lacking solid arguments, the US delegates once more resorted to their habitual "dollar diplomacy," which, as Che noted, made it impossible for Cuba to sign the Punta del Este accord.

Forty years after the Punta del Este conference, Cuban aca-
demics and researchers from various institutions participated in
a seminar, "An Alternate Project for Hemispheric Development
Workshop," which reviewed the economic and political debates
that occurred at the 1961 conference.

Dr. Ernesto Molina, professor of political economy, established a historical parallel between the positions that José Martí
took on the Pan-American and Monetary conferences that were
held in the United States in 1889 and 1891 and the statements
Che made at the Punta del Este conference, and argued for a
similar "critical analysis… of the US invitation to Our America
to subscribe to the Free Trade Area of the Americas [FTAA/
ALCA]."

Dr. Molina described the main roots of underdevelopment;
the real, objective formulas for development, such as Cuba had
proposed in 1961; and how those proposals might be a possible
model for the rest of the underdeveloped world. In this regard,
Dr. Molina said, the Alliance for Progress had been a failure,
because although it contained, temporarily, the "revolutionary
threat in the region," it did nothing to counter US hegemonic
policy.

Under present conditions, Dr. Molina said, Cuba does not
have to accept the neoliberal model to make its development
compatible with the models of integration that are being developed in the rest of Latin America. He added that, in the present conditions of economic globalization, an underdeveloped
country can only achieve development if the government regu-
lates commercial activities and if it really seeks to bring about a
progressive structural change in the economy and society with
the consensus and conscious participation of the population.

On this topic, economist and researcher Jonathan Quirós

said that not only the Alliance for Progress but the various other capitalist models of development applied in Latin America had failed and that the ideas Che set forth in Punta del Este were entirely valid today, especially those related to economic planning and to placing political power in the hands of the people.

The background Quirós presented on current reality in Latin America as the most heavily indebted region in the under-developed world showed the falseness and failure of such policies. Many experts believe that the results of this situation will be long-lasting and bring about a new wave of crises related to the region's debt. Therefore, while the Alliance for Progress proved to be a confidence trick pulled on the Latin American peoples in 1961, the FTAA has been the latest imperialist option for strengthening its power in the region with a greater degree of political and economic control and does not even offer preferential treatment for the least developed countries.

Quirós concluded the only thing that can guarantee the basic aim of integration — that of promoting economic, social, and cultural development that will impede or reduce the harmful consequences of neoliberal globalization — is a true strategy of integration among the Latin American countries, not a hegemonic project such as the FTAA.

In the sphere of economics and politics, Dr. Rosa López, a researcher and historian of Cuba-US relations, analyzed US policy toward Latin America, arguing that it passed through cycles varying from complete lack of interest to close scrutiny in a hegemonic general approach, starting with the 1945 Inter-American Conference on Problems of War and Peace to the founding of the OAS in 1948, and through to President Kennedy's 1961 Alliance for Progress.

In terms of US economic policy toward Latin America, Dr. López said the Alliance registered a slight change insofar as it included social aspects in its assistance plan in order to counter the radical alternative model of the Cuban revolution, a change which Che described as "a new instrument of economic imperialism." She added that, far from facilitating any solutions, the Alliance had produced practically no results except for increasing the military component through counterinsurgency policies to contain the advance of the liberation movements.

Considering the question of bilateral contacts, Dr. Jacinto Valdés-Dapena, a professor and researcher, discussed the informal meeting that occurred between Richard Goodwin, President Kennedy's special adviser, and Che Guevara in August 1961, after the conference was over.

In his memoirs, *Remembering America*, Goodwin described the significance of that encounter from the point of view of the historic confrontation between Cuba and the United States. Dr. Valdés-Dapena reviewed some of Goodwin's comments and discussed important aspects of the conversation: the military defeat of the United States at the Bay of Pigs; the preparation of new actions for subverting the Cuban revolution; and Cuba's significance for the Kennedy Administration as a top priority for US national security.

He pointed out that, after the Punta del Este conference, Goodwin suggestions for specific actions to be carried out against Cuba. Goodwin knew that the Kennedy Administration was working on Operation Mongoose and clearly understood from his conversation with Che that, since the 1961 Bay of Pigs attack, the foundations of the revolution had been consolidated, that Cuba's relations with the Soviet Union would increase and that socialist revolutions would be feasible in the hemisphere. So he proposed that top priority be given to the organization of an integral commando operation that would overthrow the revolution, or at least to the strengthening of the counterrevolutionary structures already in the country.

Subsequent history showed that when faced with the fact of the Cuban revolution, the US response (Operation Mongoose) was to export counterrevolution and armed insurrection to Cuba, a policy ultimately defeated by the Cuban people who were convinced that their revolution was worth fighting for.

Che's analysis of the principles of Cuba's foreign policy; the causes which led to the failure of US plans against Cuba; and the warning that if Washington's approach was not changed, more failures would follow has been borne out for over 40 years of confrontation and struggle, primarily because the United States has refused to recognize the truly Cuban, legitimate, autonomous nature of Cuban socialism.

Discussing this point, Dr. María del Carmen Ariet García, scientific coordinator of the Che Guevara Studies Center and a specialist in the life and work of Che Guevara, presented a chronological analysis of Che's meetings with presidents Arturo Frondizi, of Argentina, and Janio Quadros, of Brazil, after the Punta del Este conference and the political consequences those contacts had for the two heads of state.

Dr. Ariet compared and contrasted the two presidents, the purposes of those meetings and the risks they ran of opposition from intransigent rightists at home—risks that proved to be serious as both administrations were subsequently overthrown or defeated in other ways.

Dr. Ariet showed that, though the governments of Argentina, Brazil, and Cuba had political differences, all of them applied the basic principle of strengthening Latin America with a more independent stance, trying to avoid a worsening of the Cold War. The positions taken by presidents Frondizi and Quadros set examples of true Latin American honor.

The 2001 Havana seminar concluded with a special address by Magali Gozá León, a secretary in the Latin America Department of the Ministry of Foreign Affairs who had served as secretary of the Cuban delegation to the Punta del Este conference in 1961.

Che had remarked that all of his *compañeros* in the Cuban delegation had worked with great tenacity and done a very good job, adding that they had been models of discipline. The participants in the workshop observed that same dedication when listening to Magali Gozá's experiences, for Che had impressed his way of doing things on all of his *compañeros*.

The documents in this book succinctly reflect what happened more than 40 years ago and assist the understanding of the importance and timeliness of the Punta del Este conference and significance of the Alliance for Progress proposal. This is important, both for understanding more recent examples of the hegemonic policies the US government has tried to impose on Latin America and, above all, for understanding the full magnitude of the "new formulas" of the new millennium, in which the United States is trying to maintain its economic and political power, this time based on the requirements of globalization and neoliberalism.

In 1961, it was the Alliance for Progress; today it is the Free Trade Area of the Americas. We should remember what Che said at the Punta del Este conference, which is still the main challenge we face:

That is the world today, distinguished delegates. That is how we have to see it in order to understand this conference and draw the conclusions that will permit our peoples either to head toward a happy future of harmonious development, or else become appendages of imperialism in the preparation of a new and terrible war. Or they may shed blood in internal strife when—as almost all of you have foreseen—the people, tired of waiting, tired of being fooled once again, set out on the road that Cuba once took: that of seizing weapons from the enemy army, which represents reaction, and destroying to its very foundations a whole social order designed to exploit the people.

Che Guevara Studies Center
Havana, Cuba

Economics Cannot be Separated from Politics

Speech at Punta del Este (August 8, 1961)

Che Guevara's speech on behalf of the Cuban government to the ministerial meeting of the Inter-American Economic and Social Council (CIES),
sponsored by the Organization of American States (OAS) at Punta del
Este, Uruguay, on August 8, 1961. Head of the US delegation, Douglas
Dillon, presented Washington's recently proclaimed Alliance for Progress
for official ratification by the meeting. The conference was presided over by
Uruguayan President Eduardo Haedo.

Mr. President;

Distinguished delegates:

Like all the delegations, we must begin by expressing our
appreciation to the government and people of Uruguay for the
cordial reception they have given us during this visit.

I would also like to personally thank the distinguished
president of this gathering for the gift he made to us of the
complete works of Rodó, and would like to explain to him the
two reasons why we are not beginning this presentation with
a quotation from that great Latin American. The first is that
I went back to *Ariel* after many years, looking for a passage
that would express, at the present time, the ideas of someone

who is, more than a Uruguayan, a man of our Americas, an American from the Río Bravo to the south. But Rodó expresses throughout his *Ariel* the violent struggle and the contradictions of the Latin American peoples against the nation that 50 years ago was already interfering in our economy and in our political freedom. And it was not proper to quote this in someone else's house.

And the second reason, Mr. President, is that the head of one of the delegations here offered us a quotation from [José] Martí to begin his presentation. Well, we will answer Martí with Martí. But with the anti-imperialist and antifeudal Martí who died facing Spanish bullets, fighting for the liberty of his homeland and—as he put it in one of his last letters—trying, with Cuba's liberty, to prevent the United States from falling upon Latin America.

At that international monetary conference to which the distinguished president of the Inter-American Bank referred in his inaugural address when he spoke of the 70 years of waiting, Martí said:

> Whoever speaks of economic union speaks of political union. The nation that buys, commands; the nation that sells, serves. Commerce must be balanced to assure freedom. A nation that wants to die sells to one nation only, and a nation that would be saved sells to more than one. The excessive influence of one country over another's commerce becomes political influence. Politics is the work of men who surrender their feelings to an interest. When a strong nation supplies another with food, she requires that the recipient serve her. When a strong nation wants to engage another in battle, she forces those who have need of her to become her allies and to serve her. A nation that wants to be free must be free in matters of trade. It must

distribute its trade among nations that are equally strong. If one is to be preferred, give preference to the one who needs it the least. Let there be neither unions of the Americas against Europe, nor with Europe against a nation of the Americas. Only the mind of some university student could deduce an obligation to political union from the geographic coincidence of our living together in the Americas. Commerce follows the land and sea routes of the earth, going to whatever country has anything to exchange, be it a monarchy or a republic. Let us be in union with the whole world and not with just a part of it, not with one part against another. If the republics of the Americas have any function at all, it is certainly not to be herded by one of them against the future republics.

That was Martí 70 years ago, Mr. President.

Well, having complied with the elementary duty of honoring the dead and of repaying the kindness that the distinguished delegate has shown to us, we pass on to the fundamental part of our presentation: the analysis of why we are here, to characterize the conference. And I must say, Mr. President, that I disagree, in the name of Cuba, with almost all the statements that have been made, although I do not know if I disagree with all the private thoughts of everyone.

I must say that Cuba's interpretation is that this is a political conference. Cuba does not agree that economics can be separated from politics, and understands that they always go together. That is why you cannot have experts who speak of models when the destinies of a people are at stake. And I am also going to explain why this conference is political. It is political because all economic conferences are political; but it is also political because it was conceived against Cuba, and because it has been conceived to counter the example that Cuba represents throughout Latin America.

And if there is any doubt about that, on the 10th, in Fort Amador in the [Panama] Canal Zone, General Decker, while instructing a group of Latin American military men in the art of repressing the people, spoke of the technical conference in Montevideo and said that it had to be backed.

But that is nothing. In the inaugural message on August 5, 1961, President Kennedy asserted:

> Those of you at this conference are present at an historic moment in the life of this hemisphere. This is far more than an economic discussion, or a technical conference on development. In a very real sense it is a demonstration of the capacity of free nations to meet the human and material problems of the modern world.

I could continue quoting the prime minister of Peru, where he also refers to political themes; but in order not to tire the distinguished delegates, for I can foresee that my presentation will be a bit long, I will refer to some statements made by the "experts" — a term we place within quotation marks — on point 5 of the draft text.

At the end of page 11, it is stated as a definitive conclusion:

> To establish, on a hemispheric and national level, regular consultative procedures with the trade union advisory committees, so that they may play an influential role in the political formulation of programs that might be approved in the special session.

And to drive home my point, so no doubt can remain as to my right to speak of political matters — which is what I plan to do in the name of the Cuban government—here is a quotation from page 7 of that same report on point 5 in question:

> Delay in accepting the responsibility of democratic media to defend the essential values of our civilization, without any weakening or commitments of a material sort, would signify irreparable damage to democratic society and the imminent danger of the disappearance of the freedoms enjoyed today, as has occurred in Cuba…

Cuba is spelled out…

> …where today all newspapers, radio, television, and movies are controlled by the absolute power of the government.

In other words, distinguished delegates, in the report we are to discuss, Cuba is put on trial from a political point of view. Very well then, Cuba will state its truths from a political point of view, and from an economic point of view, as well.

We agree with only one thing in the report on point 5 by the distinguished experts, only one phrase, which defines the present situation: "A new stage is beginning in relations between the peoples of the Americas," it says, and that is true. Except that the new stage begins under the star of Cuba, free territory of the Americas. And this conference, and the special treatment that the delegations have received, and the credits that may be granted, all bear the name of Cuba, whether the beneficiaries like it or not, because a qualitative change has taken place in the Americas. A country can take up arms, destroy an oppressing army, form a new popular army, stand up to the invincible monster, wait for the monster's attack, and then defeat it. And this is something new in Latin America, gentlemen, and what makes this new language possible and what makes relations easier between everyone—except, of course, between the two great rivals of this conference.

At this time, Cuba cannot even speak of Latin America alone. Cuba is part of a world that is experiencing intense anguish because we do not know if one of the parts—the weakest, but the most aggressive—will commit the stupid mistake of unleashing a conflict that would necessarily be a nuclear one. Cuba is on the alert, distinguished delegates, because she knows that imperialism would perish enveloped in flames, but that Cuba would also suffer in its own flesh the price of imperialism's defeat, and she hopes that it can be accomplished by other means. Cuba hopes that her children will see a better future, and that victory will not have to be won at the cost of millions of human lives destroyed by the atomic bomb.

The situation of the world is tense. We are not gathered here just for Cuba—not in the least. Imperialism has to protect its rearguard because the battle is being fought on all sides, in a moment of great tension.

The Soviet Union has reaffirmed its decision to sign the Berlin peace treaty, and President Kennedy has announced that he might even go to war over Berlin. But there is not only Berlin; there is not only Cuba; there is Laos; elsewhere there is the Congo, where Lumumba was assassinated by imperialism; there is divided Vietnam; divided Korea; Formosa [Taiwan] in the hands of Chiang Kai-shek's gang; Algeria is bleeding to death, and now they also want to divide it; and there is Tunisia, whose population was machine-gunned the other day for committing the "crime" of wanting to regain their territory.

That is the world today, distinguished delegates. That is how we have to see it in order to understand this conference and draw the conclusions that will permit our peoples either to head toward a happy future of harmonious development, or else become appendages of imperialism in the preparation of a new and terrible war. Or they may shed blood in internal strife when—as almost all of you have foreseen—the people, tired of waiting, tired of being fooled once again, set out on the road that Cuba once took: that of seizing weapons from the enemy army, which represents reaction, and destroying to its very foundations a whole social order designed to exploit the people.

The history of the Cuban revolution is short in years, Mr. President, but rich in accomplishments, rich in positive accomplishments, and rich also in the bitterness of the aggressions it has suffered.

We will point out a few of them so it may be well understood that a long chain of events leads us here.

In October 1959, the only fundamental economic measure that the revolutionary government had carried out was the agrarian reform. Pirate planes coming from the United States flew over Havana's airspace and as a result of the bombs that they dropped and the fire of our antiaircraft batteries, two people were killed and 50 were wounded. Then there was the burning of the sugarcane fields, which constitutes economic aggression, an aggression against our wealth. The United States denied all responsibility until a plane blew up—pilot and all—and the origin of those pirate craft was indisputably demonstrated. This time the US government was kind enough to offer apologies. The España sugar mill was also bombed in February 1960 by these planes.

In March of that year, the steamship *La Coubre*, which was bringing arms and munitions from Belgium, exploded at the Havana docks in an accident that the experts said was intentional and that killed 100 people.

In May 1960, the conflict with imperialism became direct and sharp. The oil companies operating in Cuba, invoking the right of force and scorning the laws of the republic, which clearly specified their obligations, refused to refine the crude oil that we had bought from the Soviet Union, in the exercise of our free right to trade with the whole world and not with just a part of it, as Martí said.

Everyone knows how the Soviet Union responded, by sending us, in a real effort, hundreds of ships to annually transport 3.6 million tons—the total of our crude oil imports—to keep our whole industrial apparatus moving, which today runs on the basis of oil.

In July 1960, there was the economic aggression against Cuban sugar, although some governments have not yet recognized it as such. The contradictions became sharper and the meeting of the OAS took place in August 1960, in Costa Rica. There—in August 1960, I repeat—it was stated:

> The intervention or threat of intervention by an extra-continental power in the affairs of the American republics, even when it is invited, is strongly condemned. It is declared that the acceptance by an American state of a threat of extra-continental intervention endangers American solidarity and security, which obligates the Organization of American States to condemn and reject it with equal energy.

In other words, the sister nations of the Americas, gathered in Costa Rica, denied us the right to be defended. It is one of the strangest denials in the history of international law. Of course, our people are rather disobedient to the dictates of technical assemblies and they gathered in a great assembly of Havana, approving unanimously—with more than a million hands raised to the sky, one-sixth of the total population of the whole country—what was called the Declaration of Havana, one of whose points states:

> The National General Assembly of the People of Cuba—confident that it is expressing the general opinion of the peoples of Latin America—reaffirms that democracy is not compatible with financial oligarchy, with discrimination against Blacks and outrages by the Ku Klux Klan, or with the persecution that drove scientists like Oppenheimer from their posts, deprived the world for years of the marvelous voice of Paul Robeson, held prisoner in his own country, and sent the Rosenbergs to their deaths against the protests of a shocked world, including the appeals of many governments and of Pope Pius XII.
>
> The National General Assembly of the People of Cuba expresses the Cuban conviction that democracy cannot consist solely of elections that are nearly always fictitious and managed by rich landowners and professional politicians, but rather it lies in the right of the citizens to determine their own destiny, as this assembly of the people is now doing. Furthermore, democracy will come to exist in Latin America only when people are really free to make choices, when the poor are not reduced—by hunger, social discrimination, illiteracy, and the legal system—to the most wretched impotence...
>
> To sum up, the National General Assembly of the People of Cuba condemns: the exploitation of human by human and the exploitation of the underdeveloped countries by imperialist finance capital.

This was a declaration of our people made before the whole world, to show our resolve to defend with arms, with our blood, and with our lives, our freedom and our right to determine the destiny of our country in the way our people think best.

There followed many skirmishes and battles, verbal at times, with deeds at others, until December 1960 when the Cuban sugar quota in the US market was cut once and for all. The Soviet Union responded in the manner that you know. Other socialist countries did likewise and contracts were signed to sell to the whole socialist area four million tons of sugar, at a preferential price of four cents. That naturally saved the situation for Cuba, which unfortunately is still today as much of a one-crop country as are the majority of the countries of Latin America, and as dependent upon a single market, on a single product — at that time — as the rest of her sister countries are today.

It seemed that President Kennedy was initiating the new era that has been so talked about. And in spite of the fact that the verbal battle had been so intense between President Kennedy and the prime minister of our government, we hoped things would improve. President Kennedy in his speech issued some clear warnings on a range of Latin America issues, but he appeared to publicly accept that the case of Cuba must now be considered as a fait accompli.

We were mobilized at that time, but the day after Kennedy's speech, demobilization was ordered. Unfortunately, on March 13, 1961 — the day President Kennedy announced the Alliance for Progress — the pirate attack on our refinery at Santiago de Cuba took place, endangering the installations and taking the life of one of those defending it. We were thus again faced with an accomplished fact.

In that speech, which I have no doubt will be remembered, Kennedy also said that he hoped the peoples of Cuba and the

Dominican Republic, for whom he felt great sympathy, could join the community of free nations. Within a month there was Playa Girón [Bay of Pigs invasion], and a few days later President Trujillo was mysteriously assassinated. We were always enemies of President Trujillo; we merely take note of the bare fact, which has not been clarified in any way up to the present time.

Afterward, a true masterpiece of belligerence and political naiveté was prepared, called the White Paper. According to the magazines that chatter so much in the United States—even provoking the ire of President Kennedy—its author is one of the distinguished advisers of the US delegation that is with us today. It is an indictment filled with distortions about Cuban reality, and was conceived to prepare for what was coming.

"The revolutionary regime betrayed their own revolution," said the White Paper, as if it were the judge of revolutions and of how to make revolutions, the great appraiser of revolutions in the Americas.

"The Castro regime offers a clear and present danger to the authentic revolutions of the Americas." The word *revolution* also needs the barnacles scraped off it now and then, as one of the members presiding here said.

"The Castro regime refuses to negotiate amicably." This in spite of our having said many times that we will sit down on an equal basis to discuss our problems with the United States. I take advantage of the opportunity now, on behalf of my government, Mr. President, to state once more that Cuba is ready to sit down to discuss as equals everything that the US delegation wishes to discuss, but on the strict basis that there be no prior conditions. In other words, our position is very clear on this matter.

The White Paper calls the Cuban people to subversion and to revolution "against the Castro regime." Yet, in spite of this, on April 13 [1961], President Kennedy once more spoke and affirmed categorically that he would not invade Cuba and that the armed forces of the United States would never intervene in Cuba's internal affairs. Two days later, unmarked planes bombed our airports and reduced to ashes the greater part of our ancient air force, the remnants of what Batista's men had left behind when they fled.

In the UN Security Council, Mr. Adlai Stevenson gave emphatic assurances that they were Cuban pilots, from our air force, "unhappy with the Castro regime," who had carried out such a deed. And he stated he had spoken with them.

On April 17, the unsuccessful invasion took place. Our entire people, united and on a war footing, once more demonstrated that there are forces stronger than widespread propaganda, that there are forces stronger than the brutal force of arms, that there are higher values than the value of money. They threw themselves in a mad rush on to the narrow paths that led to the battlefield, many of them massacred on the way by the enemy's superiority in the air. Nine Cuban pilots were the heroes of that struggle, with the old planes. Two of them gave their lives; seven of them are exceptional witnesses to the triumph of freedom's weapons.

The Bay of Pigs invasion was over, and — to be brief, for there is no need to offer proof when the guilty party confesses, distinguished delegates — President Kennedy assumed full responsibility for the aggression. Perhaps at that time he did not remember the words he had spoken a few days before.

You might think that the history of aggressions was over. Nevertheless, I'll give you a scoop, as the newspaper people say. On July 26 of this year, armed counterrevolutionary groups at the Guantánamo naval base were waiting for Commander Raúl Castro at two strategic places in order to assassinate him. The plan was intelligent and macabre. They would fire upon Commander Raúl Castro while he was on the road from his house to the mass meeting at which we celebrate the date of our revolution. If they failed, they would dynamite the foundation, or rather, they would detonate the already dynamited foundations of the stand from which our *compañero* Raúl Castro would preside over that patriotic meeting. And a few hours later, distinguished delegates, US mortars would begin firing from Cuban territory against the Guantánamo naval base. So the whole world would clearly understand the matter: the Cubans, exasperated because in the midst of their personal quarrels one of those "Communists over there" was assassinated, were attacking the Guantánamo naval base, and the poor United States would have no recourse but to defend itself.

That was the plan our security forces, which are much more efficient than you might imagine, discovered a few days ago.

All that I have just told you is why I believe the Cuban revolution cannot come to this conference of illustrious experts to speak about technical matters. I know that you think, "It is because they do not know about these things." And perhaps you are right. But the fundamental thing is that politics and facts, so obstinate, which are constantly present in our situation, prevent us from coming here to speak about numbers or to analyze the perfections of the CIES specialists.

There is a series of political issues that are circulating. One of them is a political-economic question: the tractors. Five hundred tractors is not an exchange value. Five hundred tractors is what our government estimates would allow it to repair the material damage caused by the 1,200 mercenaries. They do not pay for a single life because we are not accustomed to placing a dollar value on the lives of our citizens, or a value on equipment of any kind. And much less on the lives of the children who died there, of the women who died there at the Bay of Pigs.

But we want to make it clear that if the exchange of human beings—those we call *gusanos* [worms]—for tractors seems to be an odious transaction, something from the days of piracy, we could make an exchange of human beings for human beings. We direct our remarks to the gentlemen from the United States. We reminded them of the great [Puerto Rican] patriot Pedro Albizu Campos, on the verge of death after being in a dungeon of the empire for years and years, and we offered them whatever they wanted for the freedom of Albizu Campos. We reminded the nations of the Americas who might have political prisoners in their jails that we could make an exchange. No one responded.

Naturally, we cannot force that exchange. It is simply up to those who think that the freedom of those "valiant" Cuban counterrevolutionaries—the only army in the world that surrendered in its entirety, with almost no losses—whoever thinks that these individuals should be set free, let them set free their political prisoners. Then all the jails of the Americas will be resplendent, or at least their political prisons will be empty.

There is another problem, also of a political-economic nature. This is, Mr. President, that our air transport fleet is being brought, plane by plane, to the United States. The procedure is simple: a few ladies enter a plane with guns hidden in their clothing, they hand them over to their accomplices, the accomplices murder the guard, they put a gun to the pilot's head, the pilot heads for Miami, and a company, legally of course—because in the United States everything is done legally—files a suit for debts against the Cuban government, and then the plane is confiscated.

But it so happens that among those many Cuban patriots—and in addition there was a US patriot, but he is not ours—there was a Cuban patriot [in the United States]. And he, all by himself, without anyone telling him anything, decided to better the record of the hijackers of the two-engine planes, and he brought to Cuban shores a beautiful four-engine plane. Naturally, we are not going to use this four-engine plane, which is not ours. We respect private property, but we demand the right to be respected in kind, gentlemen. We demand an end to shams; the right for there to be organizations in the Americas that can say to the United States: "Gentlemen, you are committing a vulgar outrage. You cannot take the planes of another country even though it may be opposed to you. Those planes are not yours. Return those planes, or sanctions will be imposed against you."

Naturally we understand that, unfortunately, there is no inter-American body strong enough to do this. Nevertheless, in this august conclave, we appeal to the sense of fairness and justice of the US delegation, in order to normalize the situation with regard to the hijacking of our respective planes.

It is necessary to explain what the Cuban revolution is, what this special event is that has made the blood of the world's empires boil, and that has also made the blood of the dispossessed of the world, or of this part of the world at least, boil with hope. It is an agrarian, antifeudal and anti-imperialist revolution that under the imperatives of its internal evolution and of external aggressions became transformed into a socialist revolution, and that declares itself as such before all the Americas: a socialist revolution.

A socialist revolution that took the land from those who had plenty and gave it to those who used to be hired to work that land, or distributed it in cooperatives among other groups of people who had no land on which to work, even as hired hands.

It is a revolution that came to power with its own army and on the ruins of the oppressor's army; a revolution that looked around when it came to power and dedicated itself to the systematic destruction of all the old forms of the structure that upheld the dictatorship of an exploiter class over the exploited class. It destroyed the army completely, as a caste, as an institution—not as men, except for the war criminals who were shot before a firing squad; this too was done openly before the public opinion of the continent and with a clear conscience.

It is a revolution that has reaffirmed national sovereignty and that, for the first time, has called in its own name and in the name of all the peoples of the Americas and of the world for the return of all territories unjustly occupied by foreign powers.

It is a revolution that has an independent foreign policy, that comes here to this meeting of American states as one more Latin American country, that goes to the meeting of the Non-aligned nations as one of its important members, and that participates in the deliberations of the socialist countries and is considered by them to be a fraternal nation.

It is, then, a revolution with humanist characteristics. It is in solidarity with all the oppressed peoples of the world. It is in solidarity, Mr. President, because as Martí also said:

"Every true human must feel on their own cheek every blow dealt against the cheek of another." And every time that an imperialist power subjugates a territory, it is a blow against every inhabitant of that territory.

That is why we struggle for the independence of other countries, for the independence of the occupied territories, indiscriminately, without asking about the political regime or about the aspirations of those who fight for their independence. We support Panama, which has a piece of its territory occupied by the United States. We call the islands near the south of Argentina the Malvinas and not the Falkland Islands. And we call the island that the United States snatched from Honduras and from which it is insulting us over radio and telegraph, Swan Island.

Here in the Americas we are constantly fighting for the independence of the Guianas and the British Antilles. We accept the fact of an independent Belize because Guatemala has already renounced its sovereignty over that piece of its territory. And we also fight in Africa, in Asia, in any part of the world where the strong oppress the weak, so that the weak may achieve independence, self-determination, and the right to self-rule as a sovereign state.

Permit us to say that when the earthquake struck Chile, our people came to her aid to the extent of our resources, with our only product, sugar. It was a small amount of aid, but nevertheless it was a type of aid for which nothing was demanded in return. It was simply handing over to a sister nation some food to tide her over those anxious hours. Nor does that country have to thank us, and much less does she owe us anything; it was our duty to give what we gave.

Our revolution nationalized the domestic economy; it

nationalized basic industry, including mining. It nationalized all foreign trade, which is now in the hands of the state, and which we proceeded to diversify by trading with the whole world. It nationalized the banking system in order to have in its hands the efficient instrument with which to exercise the function of credit in accordance with the country's needs.

It provides for the participation of the workers in the management of the planned national economy. It carried out the urban reform just a few months ago, through which every inhabitant of the country was made the owner of the home they occupied on the sole condition that they continue to pay the same rent that they were already paying, in accordance with a table, for a set number of years.

It instituted many measures to affirm the dignity of the human being. Among the first of these was the abolition of racial discrimination, which existed in our country, distinguished delegates, in a somewhat subtle form, but it existed. The beaches of our island were not for Blacks or the poor to swim at because they belonged to some private club visited by tourists who did not like to swim with black people.

Our hotels—Havana's great hotels, which were built by foreign companies—did not allow black people as guests, because tourists from other countries did not like it.

That is the way our country was. A woman did not have anything approaching equal rights; she was paid less for the same work; she was discriminated against, as she is in the majority of our countries.

The city and the countryside were in perpetual conflict, and from that conflict imperialism drew a work force, which was paid poorly and denied steady work.

In all these areas we carried out a revolution, and we also

carried out a true revolution in education, culture, and health care. This year illiteracy will be eliminated in Cuba. Some 104,000 literacy volunteers of all ages are spread throughout the Cuban countryside teaching reading and writing to 1.25 million illiterates, because in Cuba there were many illiterates. There were 1.25 million illiterates, many more than the official statistics used to report.

This year primary education has been made compulsory through the ninth grade, and secondary education has been made free and compulsory for the whole school-age population. We have converted the fortresses into schools. We have carried out university reform and have given the whole people free access to higher culture, to science and modern technology. We have greatly promoted national values to overcome the cultural deformation produced by imperialism, and our art receives the applause of the peoples of the world—not all the peoples, since in some places they are not allowed to enter. We have promoted the cultural heritage of Latin America through the awarding of annual prizes to writers from all latitudes of the Americas—and whose poetry prize, Mr. President, was won by the [Uruguayan] poet laureate, Roberto Ibañez, in the last contest. We have extended the social function of medicine to benefit the peasants and the poor urban workers. All the people have access to sport, to the extent that on July 25, 75,000 people marched in a sports celebration given in honor of the world's first cosmonaut, Commander Yuri Gagarin. Popular beaches have been opened to all, of course, without distinction of color or ideology, and free besides. And the exclusive social clubs of our country, of which there were many, were transformed into workers' social clubs.

All right, gentlemen experts, fellow delegates, the time has come to address the economic section of the text. Point 1 is very broad. Prepared by very brainy experts, it aims at planning the social and economic development of Latin America.

I am going to refer to some of the statements of the gentlemen experts in order to refute them from the technical point of view, and then present the Cuban delegation's viewpoint on what development planning is.

The first incongruity that we observe in this work is expressed in this passage:

> Sometimes the idea is expressed that an increase in the level and in the diversity of economic activity necessarily results in the improvement of sanitary conditions. Nevertheless, the group is of the opinion that the improvement of sanitary conditions is not only desirable per se, but that it constitutes an indispensable prerequisite to economic growth, and that it should therefore form an essential part of the programs for the development of the region.
>
> On the other hand, this is also reflected in the structure of the loans granted by the Inter-American Development Bank, for in the analysis that we made of the $120 million loaned in the first period, $40 million, in other words one-third, corresponds directly to loans of this type; for housing, for aqueducts, for sewers.

It is a bit like… I do not know, but I would almost classify it as a colonial mentality. I get the impression they are thinking of making the latrine the fundamental thing. That would improve the social conditions of the poor Indian, of the poor Black, of the poor person who lives in subhuman conditions. "Let's make latrines for them and after we have made latrines for them, and after their education has taught them how to keep themselves clean, then they can enjoy the benefits of production." Because it should be noted, distinguished delegates, that the topic of industrialization does not figure in the analysis of the distinguished experts. Planning for the gentlemen experts is the planning of latrines. As for the rest, who knows how it will be done!

If the president will allow me, I will express my deepest regrets in the name of the Cuban delegation for the loss of the services of such an efficient specialist as the one who directed this first group, Dr. Felipe Pazos. With his intelligence and capacity for work, and with our revolutionary activity, within two years Cuba could have become the paradise of the latrine, even if we did not have a single one of the 250 factories that we are beginning to build, even if we had not carried out the agrarian reform.

I ask myself, distinguished delegates, if they are not trying to make fun of us—not Cuba, because Cuba is not included, since the Alliance for Progress is not for Cuba but against her, and since it is not established to give one cent to Cuba—but if they are not trying to make fun of all the rest of the delegates.

Do you get the impression, just a little, that your leg is being pulled? You are given dollars to build highways, you are given dollars to build roads, you are given dollars to dig sewers. Gentlemen, what do you build roads with, what do you dig the sewers with, what do you build houses with? You do not have to be a genius for that. Why do not they give dollars for equipment, dollars for machinery, dollars so that our underdeveloped countries, all of them, can become industrial-agricultural countries, at one and the same time? Really, it is sad.

On page 10, in the part about development planning under point 6, it is made evident who the real author of this plan is.

Point 6 says: "To establish more solid bases for the granting and utilization of external financial aid, especially to provide effective criteria to evaluate individual projects."

We are not going to establish the most solid foundations for granting and utilization because we are not the ones granting; you are the ones who are receiving, not granting. We, Cuba, are watching, and it is the United States that is making the grants. This point 6, then, is drafted directly by the United States. It is the recommendation of the United States, and this is the spirit of the whole abortive scheme called point 1.

But I want to impress upon you one thing. We have spoken a good deal about politics. We have denounced what is a political plot here. We have emphasized in conversations with the distinguished delegates Cuba's right to express these opinions, because Cuba is directly attacked in point 5. Nevertheless, Cuba does not come here to sabotage the meeting, as some of the newspapers or many of the mouthpieces of the foreign information agencies are claiming.

Cuba comes to condemn what is worthy of condemnation from the point of view of principles. But Cuba also comes to work harmoniously, if possible, in order to straighten out this thing that has been born so distorted, and Cuba is ready to collaborate with all the distinguished delegates to set it right and make it into a beautiful project.

The honorable Mr. Douglas Dillon in his speech cited financing; that is important. We must speak of financing if we are all to get together and speak of development, and we have all assembled here to talk with the one country that has the capital for financing.

Mr. Dillon says: "Looking at the years to come and at the sources of external financing—international entities such as

Europe and Japan as much as the United States; new private investments and investments of public funds — if Latin America takes as a precondition the necessary internal measures, it can logically expect that its efforts..." He does not even say, "if it takes these measures this will happen," but only "it can logically expect"! He continues, "...will be matched by an influx of capital on the order of at least $20 billion in the next 10 years, with the majority of these funds coming from official sources."

Is this how much there is? No, only $500 million are approved; this is what is being talked about. This must be emphasized because it is the nub of the question. What does it mean? And I assure you that I'm not asking this for us, but for the good of all. What does it mean, "if Latin America takes the necessary internal measures"? And what does "it can logically expect" mean?

I think that later in the work of the committees or at a time that the representative of the United States deems opportune, this detail should be cleared up a little, because $20 billion is an interesting sum. It is no less than two-thirds of the figure that our prime minister announced as necessary for the development of the Americas; push it a little more and we arrive at $30 billion. But that $30 billion has to arrive in jingling cash, dollar by dollar, into the national coffers of each one of the countries of the Americas, with the exception of this poor Cinderella who probably will receive nothing.

That is where we can help, but not as part of a blackmail, such as is foreseen. It is said: "Cuba is the goose that lays the golden egg. Cuba exists, and while there is a Cuba, the United States will continue to give." No, we do not come here for that reason. We come to work, to try and struggle on the level of principles and ideas, for the development of our peoples. Because all or nearly all the distinguished representatives have said it: if the Alliance for Progress fails, nothing can hold back the wave of popular movements — I say this in my own words, but that is what was meant. Nothing can hold back the wave of popular movements if the Alliance for Progress fails. And we are interested in it not failing, if and insofar as it means a real improvement for Latin America in the standard of living of all its 200 million inhabitants. I can make this statement honestly and with all sincerity.

We have diagnosed and foreseen the social revolution in the Americas, the real one, because events are unfolding in a different way, because there is an attempt to hold the people back with bayonets, and when the people realize that they can take the bayonets and turn them against the ones who brandish them, then those who brandish them are lost. But if the road the people want to take is one of logical and harmonious development, through long-term loans with low interest, as Mr. Dillon said, with 50 years to pay, we also are in agreement.

The only thing is, distinguished delegates, that we all have to work together here to make that figure concrete, and to make sure that the US Congress approves it. Because do not forget that we are faced with a presidential and parliamentary regime, not a "dictatorship" like Cuba, where a representative of Cuba stands up, speaks in the name of his government, and takes responsibility for his actions. What is said here also has to be ratified over there, and the experience of all the distinguished delegates is that many times the promises made here were not approved there.

Well, what I have to say on each of these points is very long, and I'll shorten it so that we can discuss them in the commissions in a fraternal spirit. These are simply some general facts, some general considerations.

The rate of growth presented as a most beautiful thing for all Latin America is a 2.5 percent net growth. Bolivia announced 5 percent for 10 years. We congratulate the representative of Bolivia and say to him that with just a little effort and the mobilization of the popular forces he could say 10 percent. We speak of 10 percent growth with no fear whatsoever; 10 percent growth is the rate that Cuba foresees for the coming years.

What does this indicate, distinguished delegates? That if each country maintains its current course Latin America as a whole — which today has a per capita income of approximately $330 and a 2.5 percent annual growth rate — by around the year 1980 will have a per capita income of $500. Certainly for many countries that is quite phenomenal.

What does Cuba intend to have by the year 1980? A net income per capita of around $3,000; more than the United States currently has. And if you do not believe us, fine, here we are ready for a competition, gentlemen. Let us be left in peace. Let us be allowed to develop, so that we can come together again in 20 years to see if the siren song is revolutionary Cuba's or someone else's. But we are announcing, quite responsibly, that rate of annual growth.

The experts suggest the substitution of well-equipped farms for inefficient latifundia and very small farms. We say: Do they want to make an agrarian reform? Take the land from those who have a lot and give it to those who do not have any. That is the way to make an agrarian reform. The rest is a siren song. The way to do it? Whether a piece of land is given out in parcels, in accord with all the rules of private property; whether it is transformed into collective property; whether these are combined, as we have done—all that depends on the peculiarities of each nation. But agrarian reform is carried out by eliminating the latifundia, not by sending people to colonize far-off places.

In the same way I could talk about the redistribution of income, which is a reality in Cuba. Those who have more have it taken away and those who have nothing or very little are allowed to have more. Because we have made the agrarian reform. Because we have made the urban reform. Because we have reduced electrical and telephone rates—which, by the way, was the first skirmish with the foreign monopolies. Because we have made social centers for workers and child-care centers, where the children of the workers go to receive food and stay there while their parents work. Because we have created public beaches. And because we have nationalized education, which is absolutely free. In addition, we are working on an extensive health plan.

I shall speak of industrialization separately, because it is the basic foundation for development and we interpret it as such.

But there is one point that is very interesting—it is the filter, the purifier: the experts, I think there were seven—the danger of the "latrinocracy" stuck in the middle of the agreements with which the peoples want to improve their living standards. Once again, politicians in the guise of specialists, saying here yes and here no. Because you have done such and such a thing, yes, but in reality because you are a willing tool of the one who is handing out the favors. And nothing for you because you have done this wrong, but in reality because you are not a tool of the one handing out the favors—because you say, for example, that you cannot accept as the price of any loan that Cuba be attacked.

That is the danger, without mentioning that the small countries, as in everything, are the ones who receive little or nothing. Distinguished delegates, there is only one place where the small countries have the right to "kick up a fuss," and that is here, where each vote is one vote, and where this question has to be put to a vote. And the small countries, if they have a mind to, can count on the militant vote of Cuba against the measures of the "seven," measures that are "sterilized," "purified," and aimed at channeling credits, with technical disguises, in another direction.

What is the situation that really leads to authentic planning, planning that must be coordinated with everyone, but that cannot be subject to any supranational body?

We understand — and we did it this way in our country, distinguished delegates — that the precondition for real economic planning is for political power to be in the hands of the working class.

That is the *sine qua non* of genuine planning for us. Moreover, the total elimination of imperialist monopolies and state control of the fundamental productive activities are necessary. Having those three points well nailed down, you then proceed with the planning of economic development. Otherwise, everything will be lost in words, speeches, and meetings.

Besides this, there are two requirements that will decide whether or not this development makes use of the potential lying dormant in the heart of the peoples, now waiting to be awakened. These are, on the one hand, the rational, centralized direction of the economy by a single authority, which has the ability to make decisions (I'm not speaking of dictatorial powers, but the power to decide) and, on the other, the active participation of all the people in the tasks of planning.

Naturally, for the entire people to participate in the tasks of planning, they will have to own the means of production. Otherwise, it will be difficult for them to participate. The people will not want to, and it seems to me that the owners of the enterprises where they work will not want them to either.

Now, we can speak for a few minutes about what Cuba has achieved by trading with the whole world, "following the flow of commerce," as Martí said.

To date, we have signed agreements for $357 million in credits with the socialist countries, and we are in negotiations, real negotiations, for a little over $140 million more, which makes a total in loans of $500 million for the next five years.

That loan, which gives us the ownership and control of our economic development, comes to, as we said, $500 million — the sum that the United States is giving to all of Latin America — just for our little republic. This, divided by the population of the Republic of Cuba and translated to Latin America, would mean that the United States, in order to provide an equivalent amount, would have to give 15 billion pesos in five years, or $30 billion in 10 years — I speak of pesos or dollars, because in our country their value is the same. That is the sum that our prime minister asked for. With that amount, if there were a proper leadership of the economic process, Latin America in only five years would be quite a different place.

We now pass on to point 2 of the text. And naturally, before analyzing it, we will ask a political question. Some friends of ours at these meetings — of whom there are many, although it might not appear that way — were asking us if we were ready to come back into the fold of Latin American nations. We have never abandoned the Latin American nations, and we are struggling not to be expelled, not to be forced to leave the fold of Latin American republics. What we do not want is to be a herd of cattle, as Martí said. Simply that.

We denounced the dangers of the economic integration of Latin America because we are familiar with the example of Europe. In addition, Latin America knows from bitter experience what European economic integration has cost. We denounced the danger of the international monopolies completely manipulating trade relations inside the free trade associations. But we also announce here, to this conference, and we hope we are accepted, that we are willing to join the Latin American Free Trade Association, like any other member, also criticizing when necessary, but complying with all the rules, as long as Cuba's particular economic and social organization is respected and as long as its socialist government is accepted as an accomplished and irreversible fact.

In addition, equal treatment and equitable enjoyment of the advantages of the international division of labor must also be extended to Cuba. Cuba must participate actively and can contribute a great deal to alleviate many of the serious bottlenecks that exist in the economies of our countries, with the aid of the centrally managed, planned economy, and with a clear and defined goal.

Nevertheless, Cuba also proposes the following measures:

We propose the initiation of immediate bilateral negotiations for the evacuation of bases or territories in member countries occupied by other member countries, so that there are no more cases like the one reported by the delegation from Panama, where Panama's wage policy cannot be implemented in a piece of her own territory. The same is happening to us, and, speaking from the economic point of view, we would like to see that anomaly disappear.

We propose the study of rational plans of development and the coordination of technical and financial assistance from all the industrialized countries, without ideological or geographic distinctions of any kind. We also propose that guarantees be obtained to safeguard the interests of the weaker member countries; the banning of acts of economic aggression by some members against others; the guarantee of protection of Latin American entrepreneurs against the competition of foreign monopolies; the reduction of US tariffs on industrial products of the integrated Latin American countries.

And we state that, as we see it, foreign financing should take place only through indirect investments that fulfill the following conditions: that they not be subject to political demands or discriminate against state enterprises; that they be allotted in accord with the interests of the receiving country; that they carry interest rates no higher than three percent, with repayment in no less than 10 years, and renewable in case of difficulties with the balance of payments; that the attachment or confiscation of ships and aircraft by one member country against another be banned; that tax reforms be initiated that do not fall upon the working masses and that are protection against the action of foreign monopolies.

Point 3 of the text has been treated with the same delicacy as the others by the distinguished experts: they have taken up the matter with two delicate little tweezers, raised the veil a little bit, and let it fall immediately, because it is a tough one.

> It would have been desirable—*they say*—and even tempting for the group to have formulated ambitious and spectacular recommendations. However, this was not done owing to the numerous complex technical problems that would have

had to be resolved. That is why the recommendations that are formulated necessarily had to be limited to what was considered technically feasible.

I do not know if I'm being too shrewd, but reading between the lines, there do not seem to be any pronouncements. The Cuban delegation therefore proposes concretely that from this meeting we should obtain the following: a guarantee of stable prices, without any "coulds" or "might haves," without "we would examine" or "we shall examine," but, simply, guarantees of stable prices; expanding, or at least stable, markets; guarantees against economic aggression; guarantees against the unilateral suspension of purchases in traditional markets; guarantees against the dumping of subsidized agricultural surpluses; guarantees against protectionism aimed at the production of primary materials; and the creation of conditions in the industrialized countries for the purchase of primary materials with a greater degree of processing.

Cuba declares that it would be desirable for the US delegation to answer, in the commissions, whether it will continue to subsidize its production of copper, lead, zinc, sugar, cotton, wheat, and wool. Cuba asks whether the United States will continue to apply pressure against member countries to prevent them from selling their surplus primary products to the socialist countries and thus broadening their market.

And now comes point 5 of the text, since point 4 is nothing but a report. This point 5 is the other side of the coin.

Fidel Castro said at the time of the Costa Rica conference that the United States had gone there "with a sack of gold in one hand and a club in the other." Here today, the United States comes with the sack of gold — fortunately even bigger — in one hand, and the barrier to isolate Cuba in the other. It is, anyway, a triumph of historical circumstances.

But point 5 of the text establishes a program of measures for Latin America aimed at the regimentation of thought, the subordination of the trade union movement, and, if possible, the preparation of military aggression against Cuba.

Three steps are contemplated throughout the whole document: the mobilization, beginning immediately, of the Latin American mass media against the Cuban revolution and against the struggles of our peoples for their freedom; the formation at a later meeting of an inter-American federation of press, radio, television, and cinema, which would allow the United States to direct the policy of all the organs of public opinion in Latin America, of all of them—there are not many now that are outside their sphere of influence, but they want all of them. In addition, they want to exercise monopoly control over new information agencies and to absorb as many of the old ones as possible.

All this, in order to do something unprecedented, which has been announced here with such tranquility and which in my country provoked deep discussion when something similar was done in only one case. They are attempting, distinguished delegates, to establish a cultural common market, organized, managed, paid for, and domesticated. All the culture of Latin America at the service of imperialism's propaganda plans, to demonstrate that the hunger of our peoples is not hunger at all, but laziness. Magnificent!

Confronted with this, we reply: a call must be made to the organs of public opinion in Latin America, that they take up and share in the ideals of national liberation of each Latin American people. There must be a call for the exchange of information, cultural media, organs of the press, and the attainment of direct visits without discrimination between our peoples, gentlemen, because today a US citizen who goes to Cuba faces five years in prison when they return to their country. A call must be made to the Latin American governments for them to guarantee the freedoms that allow the working class movement to organize independent trade unions, to defend the interests of the workers, and to struggle for the true independence of its peoples. And we call for a total, absolute condemnation of point 5 as an attempt by imperialism to domesticate the one thing that our peoples had been saving from disaster: the national culture.

Distinguished delegates, permit me to give an outline of the objectives of Cuba's first plan of economic development for the next four-year period. The overall rate of growth will be 12 percent, that is to say, more than 9.5 percent net per capita growth, transforming Cuba into the most industrial country in Latin America in relation to its population, as the following data indicates:

First place in Latin America in per capita production of steel, cement, electrical energy and, except for Venezuela, oil refining. First place in Latin America in tractors, rayon, footwear, textiles, etc. Second place in the world in the production of metallic nickel (up until now Cuba had only produced concentrates); the production of nickel in 1965 will be 70,000 metric tons, which constitutes approximately 30 percent of the world's production. In addition, Cuba will produce 2,600 metric tons of metallic cobalt. The production of 8.5 to 9 million tons of sugar. The beginning of the transformation of the sugar industry into a sucro-chemical industry.

In order to accomplish these measures — which are easy

to list but demand enormous work and the effort of an entire people in order to succeed, plus a great deal of external financing for the purpose of aid and not exploitation—the following measures have been taken: more than a billion pesos (the Cuban peso is equivalent to the dollar) are going to be invested in industry in the installation of 800 megawatts of electrical generating capacity. In 1960, the installed capacity—not counting the sugar industry, which works seasonally—was 621 megawatts. Building or expanding 205 factories, among which the following 22 are the most important: a new plant to refine metallic nickel, which will raise the total to 70,000 tons; a petroleum refinery with a capacity of two million tons of crude oil; the first steel plant, for 700,000 tons, which in this four-year period will produce 500,000 tons of steel; the expansion of our seamed steel-pipe plants to produce 25,000 metric tons; tractors, 5,000 units annually; motorcycles, 10,000 units annually; three cement plants and the expansion of the existing ones for a total of 1.5 million metric tons, which will raise our production to 2.5 million tons annually; metal containers: 291 million units; expansion of our glass factories to 23,700 metric tons annually; a million square meters of window glass; a new factory for making 10,000 cubic meters of plywood from bagasse; a plant for making 60,000 metric tons of bagasse cellulose, in addition to one for wood cellulose of 40,000 metric tons annually; a 60,000-ton ammonium nitrate plant; 60,000 tons of simple superphosphate; 81,000 metric tons of triple superphosphate; 132,000 metric tons of nitric acid; 85,000 metric tons of ammonia; eight new textile plants and the expansion of the existing ones with 451,000 spindles; a kenaf sack factory producing 16 million sacks. And there are other factories of less importance, for a total of 205 to date.

These credits have been contracted for, up until now, in the following way: $200 million with the Soviet Union; $60 million with the People's Republic of China; $40 million with the Socialist Republic of Czechoslovakia; $15 million with the Romanian People's Republic; $15 million with the Hungarian People's Republic; $12 million with the Polish People's Republic; $10 million with the German Democratic Republic and $5 million with the Bulgarian Democratic Republic. The total contracted for to date is $357 million. The new negotiations that we expect will shortly conclude are mostly with the Soviet Union, which, as the most industrialized country in the socialist area, is the one that has offered the most extensive support.

In terms of agriculture, Cuba has set itself the goal of reaching self-sufficiency in the production of food, including fats and rice, not wheat; self-sufficiency in cotton and coarse fibers; the creation of exportable surpluses of tropical fruits and other agricultural products, whose contribution to exports will triple the present levels.

As regards foreign trade: the value of exports will increase by 75 percent over 1960; diversification of the economy — sugar and its derivatives will make up about 60 percent of the value of the exports, and not 80 percent as now.

As regards construction: the elimination of 40 percent of the present housing shortage, including the *bohíos,* which are Cuban huts; the rational combination of construction materials to increase the use of local materials without sacrificing quality.

There is one point I would like to spend a minute on: that is education. We have laughed at the group of experts who would put education and sanitation as the condition *sine qua non* to begin the path of development. This seems to us to be an aberration, but that does not make it less true that once the path of development is taken, education must proceed parallel with it. Without an adequate technological education, development is retarded. Therefore, Cuba has carried out a complete reform of education. It has expanded and improved educational services and has developed an overall educational plan.

At present Cuba occupies first place in Latin America in the allocation of resources to education: 5.3 percent of the national income. The developed nations devote 3 to 4 percent and Latin America from 1 to 2 percent of their national income to education. In Cuba, 28.3 percent of the current expenses of the state are for the Ministry of Education. Including other organizations that dedicate financial resources for education, that percentage rises to 30 percent. Among the Latin American countries, the next highest allocates 21 percent of its budget.

An increase in the budget to education, from $75 million in 1958 to $128 million in 1961, is an increase of 71 percent. The total expenses for education, including the literacy campaign and building schools, come to $170 million, 25 pesos per capita. In Denmark, for example, $25 per capita a year are spent on education; in France, $15; in Latin America, $5.

The creation, in two years, of 10,000 schoolrooms and the appointment of 10,000 new teachers. Cuba is the first country in Latin America that fully satisfies the needs of primary instruction for the entire student population, an aspiration of the principal project of UNESCO in Latin America for 1968, already achieved today in Cuba.

These really marvelous accomplishments and figures, absolutely true, that we present here, distinguished delegates, have been made possible by the following measures: the nationalization of instruction, making it secular and free, and allowing complete utilization of its services; the creation of a system of scholarships, which guarantees meeting all the students' needs, in accordance with the following plan: 20,000 scholarships for basic secondary schools from seventh to ninth grade; 3,000 for the pre-university institutes; 3,000 for art instructors; 6,000 for universities; 1,500 for courses in artificial insemination; 1,200 for courses in agricultural machinery; 14,000 for courses in tailoring and sewing and home economics for peasant women; 1,200 for the training of rural school teachers; 750 for introductory courses in elementary education; 10,000 scholarships and study stipends for students of technological education; and, in addition, hundreds of scholarships to study technology in the socialist countries; the creation of 100 centers of secondary education, with each municipality having at least one.

This year in Cuba, as I announced, illiteracy is being wiped out. It is a marvelous sight. Up to the present moment, 104,500 *brigadistas*, almost all of them students between 10 and 18 years old, have flooded the country from one end to the other, going directly to the peasant's *bohío*, to the worker's house, to convince the old person who does not want to study anymore, and thus to wipe out illiteracy in Cuba.

Each time a factory eliminates illiteracy among its workers, it raises a flag announcing this fact to the people of Cuba. Each time a cooperative wipes out illiteracy among its peasants, it hoists the same standard. And the 104,500 young students have as their symbol a book and a lantern, to bring the light of learning to the backward regions. They belong to the Conrado Benítez brigades, named in honor of the first martyr for education in the Cuban revolution, who was lynched by a group of counterrevolutionaries for the grave crime of teaching the peasants in the mountains of our country to read.

That is the difference, distinguished delegates, between our country and those who combat us. A total of 156,000 literacy volunteers, who are not full-time since they are workers or professionals, are working in education; 32,000 teachers are leading this army. And only with the active cooperation of all the Cuban people are they able to achieve such significant statistics.

All this has been done in one year, or rather, in two years; seven regimental barracks have been converted into school-cities; 27 barracks into schools; and all this while facing the danger of imperialist aggression. The Camilo Cienfuegos School-City today has 5,000 pupils from the Sierra Maestra, and units are under construction for 20,000 pupils. The construction of a similar school-city in each province is projected. Each school-city will be self-sufficient in foodstuffs, introducing peasant children to agricultural techniques.

Moreover, new methods of teaching have been established. From 1958 to 1959, primary school enrollment increased from 602,000 to 1,231,700 pupils; basic secondary school, from 21,900 to 83,800; commercial schools, from 8,900 to 21,300; technical schools, from 5,600 to 11,500.

A total of $48 million has been invested in school construction in only two years. The National Printing Plant guarantees textbooks and other printed matter for all students, free of charge. There are two television networks that cover the whole national territory, and we use that powerful media for the massive dissemination of learning. Likewise, the entire national radio is at the disposal of the Ministry of Education. The Cuban Institute of Cinematographic Art and Industry, the National Library, and the National Theater, with departments throughout the country, complete the great apparatus for the dissemination of culture. The National Institute of Sports, Physical Education, and Recreation, whose initials are INDER, promotes physical development on a mass scale.

This, distinguished delegates, is the cultural panorama of Cuba at this time.

Now comes the final part of our presentation, the part of definitions, because we want to make our position completely clear.

We have denounced the Alliance for Progress as a vehicle designed to separate the people of Cuba from the other peoples of Latin America, to sterilize the example of the Cuban revolution, and then to subdue the other peoples according to imperialism's instructions. I would like to be allowed to fully demonstrate this.

There are many interesting documents in the world. We shall distribute among the delegates some documents that came into our hands and that demonstrate, for example, the opinion that imperialism has of the Venezuelan government, whose foreign minister harshly attacked us a few days ago, perhaps because he thought we were violating rules of friendship with his people or his government.

Nevertheless, it is interesting to point out that friendly hands brought us an interesting document. It is a report of a secret document addressed to Ambassador Moscoso in Venezuela by his advisers John M. Cates, Jr., Irving Tragen, and Robert Cox.

In one of the paragraphs, speaking of the measures that must be taken in Venezuela to make a real Alliance for Progress directed by the United States, this document states:

Reform of the bureaucracy: All the plans that are formulated...

They are speaking of Venezuela.

> ...all the programs that are initiated for the economic deve-
> lopment of Venezuela, whether they be by the Venezuelan
> government or by US experts, will have to be put into practice
> through the Venezuelan bureaucracy. But as long as the public
> administration of this country is characterized by incompetence,
> indifference, inefficiency, formalism, factional favoritism in the
> granting of jobs, theft, duplication of functions, and the creation
> of private empires, it will be practically impossible to put into
> effect dynamic and efficient projects through the governmental
> machinery. For that reason the reform of the administrative
> apparatus is possibly now the most fundamental necessity,
> which is not only directed to correcting basic economic and
> social injustice, but which also could imply reconditioning
> the very instrument by which all the other basic reforms and
> development projects will be molded.

There are many interesting things in this document that we
will put at the disposal of the distinguished delegates, in which
they speak, also, of the natives. After teaching the natives, they
let the natives work. We are natives, nothing more. But there is
something very interesting, distinguished delegates, and that
is the recommendation that Mr. Cates makes to Mr. Moscoso
about what must be done in Venezuela and why it must be
done. He says as follows:

> The United States will be faced with the necessity, probably
> sooner than it is thought, of pointing out to the conservatives,
> the oligarchy, the newly rich, the national and foreign moneyed
> sectors in general, the military, and the clergy, that they will
> in the last analysis have to choose between two things: to
> contribute to the establishment in Venezuela of a society based

on the masses, in which they retain part of their status quo and wealth, or to be faced with the loss of both (and very possibly their own death at the hands of a firing squad)…

This is a report of the US advisers to their ambassador.

> …if the forces of moderation and progress are routed in Venezuela.

After this, we are given the complete picture of the whole deception to be practiced in this conference, with other reports of the secret instructions given in Latin America by the US State Department in reference to the "Cuba case."

This is very important, because it is what exposes the wolf in sheep's clothing. This is what it says. I am goin؞ to read an extract in deference to the brevity that I have already violated, but afterward we will circulate all of it:

> From the beginning, it was widely taken for granted in Latin America that the invasion was backed by the United States and, for that reason would be successful. The majority of the governments and responsible sections of the population were prepared to accept a fait accompli, although there were misgivings about the violation of the principle of non-intervention.
>
> The communists and other vehemently pro-Castro elements immediately took the offensive with demonstrations and acts of violence directed against US agencies in various countries, especially in Argentina, Bolivia and Mexico. Nevertheless, such anti-US and pro-Castro activities received limited backing and had less effect than might have been expected.
>
> The failure of the invasion discouraged the anti-Castro sectors, who thought that the United States should have done

something dramatic that would restore its damaged prestige, but it was received with joy by the communists and other pro-Castro elements.

It continues:

In most cases, the reactions of the Latin American governments were not surprising. With the exception of Haiti and the Dominican Republic, the republics that had already broken or suspended their relations with Cuba expressed their understanding of the US position. Honduras joined the anti-Castro camp, suspending its relations in April and proposing the formation of an alliance of Central American and Caribbean nations to deal with Cuba through force. The proposal, which was also suggested independently by Nicaragua, was quietly abandoned when Venezuela refused to back it.

Venezuela, Colombia, and Panama expressed a serious concern about Soviet and international communist penetration in Cuba, but they remained in favor of carrying out some type of collective action by the OAS to deal with the Cuban problem.

"Collective action by the OAS" — here we enter familiar territory.

A similar opinion was adopted by Argentina, Uruguay, and Costa Rica. Chile, Ecuador, Bolivia, Brazil, and Mexico refused to back any position that might imply an intervention in the internal affairs of Cuba. This attitude was probably very strong in Chile, where the government met strong opposition in all spheres to an open military intervention by any state against the Castro regime. In Brazil and Ecuador the question provoked serious divisions in the cabinet, in the congress, and in the political parties.

In the case of Ecuador, the intransigently pro-Cuba position of President Velasco was shaken but not altered by the discovery that Ecuadoran communists were being trained inside the country in guerrilla tactics by pro-Castro revolutionaries.

Parenthetically, I will state that this is a lie.

Likewise, there is little doubt that some of the formerly uncommitted elements in Latin America have been favorably impressed by Castro's ability to survive a military attack supported by the United States against his regime. Many who had hesitated to commit themselves before, because they believed that the United States would eliminate the Castro regime in the course of time, may have changed their opinion now. The victory of Castro has demonstrated to them the permanent and viable character of the Cuban revolution.

This is the report by the United States.

Moreover, his victory has undoubtedly aroused the latent anti-US attitude that prevails in a great part of Latin America.

In all respects, the member states of the OAS are now less hostile to US intervention in Cuba than before the invasion, but a majority—including Brazil and Mexico, who together account for more than half the population of Latin America—are not ready to actively intervene or even to join in a quarantine against Cuba. Nor could it be expected that the OAS would give beforehand its approval of direct intervention by the United States, except in the event that Castro might be involved, beyond any doubt, in an attack on a Latin American government.

Even when the United States might be successful...

Which looks improbable.

> ...in persuading the majority of Latin American states to join in a quarantine of Cuba, it would not be totally successful. Certainly Mexico and Brazil would refuse to cooperate and would serve as a channel for travel and other communication between Latin America and Cuba.
>
> Mexico's long-standing opposition to intervention of any kind would not represent an insuperable obstacle to collective action by the OAS against Cuba. The attitude of Brazil, however, which exercises a strong influence over its South American neighbors, is decisive for hemispheric cooperation. As long as Brazil refuses to act against Castro, it is probable that a number of other nations, including Argentina and Chile, would not want to risk adverse internal repercussions to accommodate the United States.
>
> The magnitude of the threat that Castro and the communists constitute in other parts of Latin America will probably continue to depend, fundamentally, on the following factors: (a) the ability of the regime to maintain its position; (b) its efficacy in demonstrating the success of its mode of coping with the problems of reform and development; and (c) the ability of the noncommunist elements in other Latin American countries to provide feasible and popularly acceptable alternatives.
>
> If, by means of propaganda, etc., Castro can convince the disaffected elements of Latin America that basic social reforms are really being made...

That is to say, if the distinguished delegates are convinced that what we are saying is true.

> ...that benefit the poorest classes, the attraction of the Cuban example will increase and will continue to inspire imitators on

the left in the whole region. The danger is not so much that a subversive apparatus, with its center in Havana, could export revolution, as that growing extreme poverty and discontent among the masses of the Latin American people may provide the pro-Castro elements opportunities to act.

After considering whether or not we are intervening, they argue:

> It is probable that the Cubans will act cautiously in this respect for some time. Probably they do not wish to risk the interception or discovery of any military adventure or military supply operation originating in Cuba. Such an eventuality would lead to a hardening of official Latin American opinion against Cuba, possibly to the point of providing tacit support to US intervention, or at least giving possible motives for sanctions on the part of the OAS. For these reasons and owing to Castro's concern with the defense of his own territory at this time, the use of Cuban military forces to support insurrection in other places is extremely improbable.

So, distinguished delegates who might have doubts, the government of the United States is announcing that it is very difficult for our troops to interfere in the internal affairs of other countries.

> As time goes on, and with the absence of direct Cuban intervention in the internal affairs of neighboring states, the present fears of Castroism, of Soviet intervention in the regime, of its "socialist" nature...

They put it in quotation marks.

> ...and of repugnancy for the repression of Castro's police

> state, will tend to decrease and the traditional policy of non-intervention will reassert itself.

It says further on:

> Apart from its direct effect on the prestige of the United States in that area...

Which undoubtedly has decreased as a result of the failure of the invasion.

> ...the survival of the Castro regime could have a profound effect on Latin American political life in coming years. Likewise, it prepares the scene for a political struggle in the terms promoted by communist propaganda for a long time in this hemisphere, with the anti-United States, "popular"...

In quotation marks.

> ...forces on one side, and the ruling groups allied to the United States on the other. The governments that promise an evolutionary reform over a period of years, even at an accelerated pace, will be confronted by political leaders who promise an immediate remedy for the social ills by means of the confiscation of property and the overturning of the society. The most immediate danger of Castro's army for Latin America could very well be the danger to the stability of those governments that are presently attempting evolutionary social and economic changes, rather than to those that have tried to prevent such changes, in part due to the tensions and heightened expectations that accompany social changes and economic development. The urban unemployed and the landless peasants of Venezuela and Peru, for example, who have hoped that Acción Democrática and the APRA would

implement reforms, constitute a quick source of political strength for the politician who convinces them that change can be implemented much more rapidly than the social democratic movements have promised. The popular support that the groups seeking evolutionary changes presently enjoy or the potential backing that they normally could obtain as the Latin American masses become more active politically would be lost to the degree that the extremist political leaders, utilizing the example of Castro, can rally support for revolutionary change.

And in the last paragraph, gentlemen, appears our friend who is present here:

> The Alliance for Progress could very well provide the stimulus to carry out more intensive reform programs. But unless these are initiated rapidly and begin soon to show positive results, it is probable that they will not be sufficient to counterbalance the growing pressure of the extreme left. The years ahead will witness, almost surely, a race between those who are attempting to initiate evolutionary reform programs and those who are trying to generate mass support for fundamental economic and social revolution. If the moderates are left behind in this race they could, in time, see themselves deprived of their mass support and caught in an untenable position between the extremes of right and left.

These are, distinguished delegates, the documents the Cuban delegation wanted to place before you, in order to analyze frankly the Alliance for Progress. Now we all know the private judgment of the US State Department: the economies of the Latin American countries have to grow because if they do not a phenomenon called Castroism will come to the fore, which will be dreadful for the United States.

Well then, gentlemen, let us make the Alliance for Progress on those terms: let the economies of all the member countries of the OAS really grow. Let them grow so that they consume their own products and not so that they are turned into a source of income for the US monopolies. Let them grow to assure social peace, not to create new reserves for an eventual war of conquest. Let them grow for us, not for those abroad.

And to all of you, distinguished delegates, the Cuban delegation says with all frankness: we wish, on our conditions, to be within the Latin American family. We want to live with Latin America. We want to see you grow, if possible, at the same rate that we are growing, but we do not oppose your growing at another rate. What we do demand is the guarantee of nonaggression for our borders.

We cannot stop exporting our example, as the United States wants, because an example is something intangible that crosses borders. What we do guarantee is that we will not export revolution. We guarantee that not one rifle will be moved from Cuba, that not one weapon will be moved from Cuba for fighting in any other country in Latin America.

What we cannot guarantee is that the idea of Cuba will not take root in some other country of Latin America, and what we do guarantee this conference is that if urgent measures of social prevention are not taken, the example of Cuba will take root in the people. And then that statement that once gave people a lot to think about, which Fidel made one July 26 and which was interpreted as an aggression, will again be true. Fidel said that if the social conditions continued as they have been until now, "the Andes would become the Sierra Maestra of Latin America."

Distinguished delegates, we call for an Alliance for Progress, an alliance for our progress, a peaceful alliance for the progress of all. We are not opposed to being left out in the distribution of loans, but we are opposed to being left out in participating in the cultural and spiritual life of our Latin American people, to whom we belong.

What we will never allow is a restriction on our freedom to trade and have relations with all the peoples of the world. And we will defend ourselves with all our strength against any attempt at foreign aggression, be it from an imperial power or be it from some Latin American body that concurs in the desire of some to see us wiped out.

To conclude, Mr. President, distinguished delegates, I want to tell you that some time ago we had a meeting of the general staff of the Revolutionary Armed Forces in my country, a general staff to which I belong. An aggression against Cuba was being discussed, which we knew would come, but we did not know when or where. We thought it would be very big; in fact, it was going to be very big. This happened prior to the famous warning of the prime minister of the Soviet Union, Nikita Khrushchev, that their rockets could fly beyond the Soviet borders. We had not asked for that aid and we did not know about their readiness to aid us. Therefore, we met knowing that the invasion was coming, in order to face our final destiny as revolutionaries.

We knew that if the United States invaded Cuba, there would be a massive slaughter, but that in the end we would be defeated and expelled from every inhabited place in the country. We members of the general staff then proposed that Fidel Castro retire to a secure place in the mountains and that one of us take charge of the defense of Havana. Our prime minister and leader answered at that time with words that exalt him, as do all his actions—that if the United States invaded Cuba and Havana was defended as it should be defended, hundreds of thousands of men, women and children would be slaughtered by Yankee weapons, and the leader of a people in revolution could not be asked to take shelter in the mountains; that his place was there, where the cherished dead were to be found, and that there, with them, he would fulfill his historic mission.

That invasion did not take place, but we maintain that spirit, distinguished delegates. For that reason I can predict that the Cuban revolution is invincible, because it has a people and because it has a leader like the one leading Cuba.

That is all, distinguished delegates.

The Real Road to Development

Second Speech at Punta del Este (August 16, 1961)

Che Guevara, representing the Cuban revolutionary government, gave this second speech at the 7th Plenary Session of the Special Meeting of the Inter-American Economic and Social Council (CIES), at Punta del Este on August 16, 1961.

Mr. President and fellow delegates:

Cuba is forced to abstain in the general vote on the document. I would like to give some details to explain why it is doing so.

Mr. President, in the speech that this delegation gave during the inaugural session, we warned of the dangers that the Alliance for Progress meeting entailed, believing that it was the beginning of a maneuver aimed at isolating the Cuban revolution.

Even so, the Cuban delegation explained that it was willing to work harmoniously, to discuss matters in line with the guiding principles of our revolution and to try to coordinate joint action with all countries in order to achieve documents that would express not only our peoples' reality but also their aspirations.

Unfortunately, the Cuban delegation understands that it has not been possible to fulfill those aspirations in full. Mr. President, Cuba brought 29 draft resolutions on many of the main problems that, in our view, afflict Latin America, distort its development and force it to do what the foreign monopolies want.

Cuba pointed out the contradiction between the insignificance of the goals and the magnificence of the proclamations. The participants talked of a challenge to the future; they talked of an alliance that was going to provide Latin America with well-being, and many grandiloquent words were employed.

However, when it comes to saying precisely which decade will be the one of democratic progress, we find that, at a net annual per capita growth rate of 2.5 percent, it will take around 100 years to reach the present level of the United States— which, clearly, has a high standard of living—but it is not an unattainable goal that should be considered absurd for the countries of Latin America and the rest of the world.

Moreover, calculating—naturally, this is a calculation that does not have a scientific basis and serves only as a means of expressing ideas—that the development process of the countries that are presently underdeveloped and that of the industrialized countries remains the same, it would take the underdeveloped countries 500 years to achieve the same per capita income as in the developed countries. We understand that, when the situation in Latin America is like this—and there is a reason for our having held this economic conference—we cannot talk about such grand purposes while setting such small goals for ourselves.

In education and health, the goals have also been very modest—in some cases more modest than the proposals that international organizations, such as UNESCO, set several years ago. Our country has more than met some of these goals, and it will more than meet all of them within the next five years.

No goals were defined in housing, and we did not even come up with a qualitative definition of what the region's industrial development will be.

Moreover, we have noted some lack of precision in setting goals in agriculture, where large and small landholdings are treated the same way and where the activities of the foreigners who have large landholdings—which distort the economies of many Latin American countries—are not even considered.

Cuba felt that if many of these goals, which had already been stated, were left in more or less the same form as in the original documents that were submitted to us for our consideration and, if the system of direct private investments from abroad was maintained, it would be impossible to attain the fundamentals required for really establishing the right of the Latin American peoples to begin: their right to lay the foundations of the healthy economies required for achieving high growth rates.

In addition, during the conference, the Cuban delegation repeatedly asked what mechanism would be used for distributing the resources of the so-called Alliance for Progress and if Cuba would have access to those resources. These two questions have not been answered.

With regard to Latin American economic integration, Cuba pointed out that integration was not a panacea and could not serve as an alternative to basic socioeconomic reforms, and it asked if countries with different forms of economic and social organization would be included in that integration, since Cuba was willing to support Latin American integration if its specific socioeconomic characteristics were respected.

Moreover, Cuba pointed out that full territorial sovereignty was a prerequisite for solid integration and referred specifically to the Guantánamo Naval Base that exists in Cuban territory, as well as to the Panama Canal. In addition, some further requests were made — requests that were sometimes whittled down considerably from their original form — which were incorporated in one way or another in the meeting's final documents. But others, such as the demand for guarantees for the ships and planes of all the member countries, were not even taken up.

With regard to raw materials and commodities, we pointed to the instability of prices and markets; denounced economic aggression and asked that it be condemned and proscribed; pointed to the need for the Latin American countries to diversify their exports, increasing the processing of raw materials and commodities, incorporating new products in their exports and opening new markets; and specifically pointed to the market of the socialist world, which now has a global growth rate of 10 percent.

Cuba criticized subsidies and the dumping of raw materials and commodities by the industrialized countries and pointed to the risks that the accumulation of agricultural surpluses or strategic mineral reserves may bring to the raw materials and commodities markets. Cuba's proposals and warnings were echoed by some countries, and it echoed those of other countries in some cases because, naturally, many of these problems are common to our underdeveloped countries.

However, the final document has reduced the real intentions of the promoters of these ideas to practically nothing, just pulling teeth. For example, while the Cuban delegation urged that restrictions on imports and subsidies for the domestic production of raw materials and commodities by the industrialized countries be abolished, the final document spoke only of reducing those restrictions until they were abolished, "if possible."

The same thing happened with many other specific proposals, all of them ending up as vague declarations including the phrases "if possible," "within the regulations," "conditions permitting," "if so required" and "if permitted." Thus, the escape clauses have already been established.

According to the [UN] Food and Agriculture Organization, the United States spent — this is what is stated in the data I have — US$2.525 billion to support agricultural prices in 1955. This is much more than the amount it has given in any one year to the countries in the Alliance for Progress.

This document does not even offer an effective guarantee that subsidized production in the United States will not continue to expand.

Cuba participated constructively in many proposals, trying to achieve effective resolutions that, without infringing on the sovereignty of any member country — not even the sovereignty of that powerful country which, because of its industrial development, is in a different situation than the others — could lead to an understanding that would give the smaller and underdeveloped countries in general full guarantees that they could initiate that new era so many people are talking about.

Yesterday, the declaration that we worked on and on which Cuba abstained because it contains several debatable points — some of them basic and others a matter of wording, as had happened throughout the meeting — was presented.

The main point is that, once again, the United States did not reply to Cuba's question, so its silence should be interpreted as a negative, and Cuba will not take part in the Alliance for Progress. You cannot support an alliance in which one of the allies will not have any participation. In addition, the declaration does not attack the main root of our ills — the existence of foreign monopolies that distort our economies and even tie our international policies to dictates from abroad.

It does not denounce economic aggression, and Cuba, which knows from its own experience just how harmful such aggression is, feels that it is very important to denounce that aggression.

The declaration insists on solving Latin America's problems by means of monetary policy, assuming that monetary changes will change the countries' economic structures. We have stated over and over again that a complete structural change in the relations of production is required in order to create the conditions that must exist if the peoples are to make any progress.

It also remains within a free enterprise framework, which Cuba has publicly condemned in philosophical terms, together with the exploitation of human by human. In practice, free enterprise, which has nothing to do with the new development processes, has been nearly eliminated in our territory.

Fellow delegates, these are the reasons why Cuba cannot sign this document.

However, I would like to say that some constructive work has been done and that Cuba has not felt isolated during this conference. Many meetings were held to which Cuba was not invited — and, naturally, we cannot express an opinion on the content of the discussions that took place. But we do know that the main topic in many of them was Cuba, and we also know that there were good friends, people holding strong convictions and positions, who maintained an attitude favorable to Cuba.

So, we have reached the final session of this conference in harmony, and we believe that we have shown that, at all times, we sought to cooperate in expanding the inter-American system on the basis of real independence and friendship with the peoples—not on the basis of making all of us dependent, under the orders of one.

Cuba has been satisfied with the proceedings here, insofar as we think new perspectives are opening for Latin America, even though our delegation could not sign the document.

One of the paragraphs explicitly admits the existence of systems that are different from those based on the philosophy of free enterprise; therefore, it admits that this meeting includes a country that has some specific characteristics that differentiate it from the others but that still allow it to be part of the whole, since it is explicitly defined in one of the "whereases."

Therefore, we think that the first link of true peaceful coexistence in the Americas has been established and that the first step has been taken for those governments that are resolutely opposed to our government and to our system at least to acknowledge the irreversibility of the Cuban revolution and its right to be recognized as an independent government, with all of its specific characteristics—even though they do not like its system of government.

The US government has voted for all the parts of this document, and we understand that it has also taken a positive step, establishing that regimes may exist whose philosophy adversely affects that of free enterprise in this part of the Americas. We think this is a very positive step.

We have always been willing to settle our differences with the US government—differences that have given rise to a lot of discussion and to some meetings in this part of the world — and we have always said that we can meet anywhere, as long as there are no strings attached.

Once more, our government expressly states this willingness. It also states that it is not begging for any kind of rapprochement or asking for a truce; rather, it is simply stating its position and letting all the friendly countries know clearly that Cuba wants to live in peace with all the peoples of the Americas that want to do the same.

However, we believe that there is still a danger. We would fail to uphold the Cuban revolution's tradition of being totally forthright if we did not say that we know that all those meetings were somehow linked to a meeting of foreign ministers in which the case of Cuba was discussed. We understand that a lot of traveling has been done in this regard, seeking affirmative votes for the meeting.

Nevertheless, something constructive has been achieved. Years ago, the foreign ministers met to denounce Guatemala, and then an economic conference was promised. More or less the same thing happened with Costa Rica. Now, an economic conference is being held, and the foreign ministers will later meet.

We think that this is a great step forward, and we hope that the foreign ministers' meeting will not be held; if it is not, that would constitute an even bigger step forward. But now the main dilemma of this era has been posed; this is a crucial moment for the peoples of the world, one whose importance is also reflected in the Americas.

Several delegates — maybe all of you — have wondered, "What will happen if the Alliance for Progress fails?" This is a very important question. The United States has felt the pressure exerted by the peoples. It has seen that the situation in Latin America, as in the rest of the world, is one of extreme tension; that it threatens the very foundations of the imperialist regime; and that we must seek a solution.

This Alliance for Progress is an attempt to seek a solution within the framework of economic imperialism. We believe that, in these conditions, the Alliance for Progress will be a failure. First of all, without any desire to offend, I doubt that it will have US$20 billion to work with in the next few years. The administrative restrictions of the great country to the north are such that it sometimes threatens — as I think it is doing today — to attach strings to foreign loans of as little as US$5 million. If that threat exists for such small amounts, you can imagine the threats there will be for amounts as large as the one already mentioned.

Moreover, it has been stated explicitly that those loans will be used mainly to promote free enterprise. And, since the imperialist monopolies that have been consolidated in almost all Latin American countries have not been denounced in any way, it is logical to suppose that the loans that are agreed to will be used to develop those monopolies. Unquestionably, this will bring about an upsurge in industry and business and result in profits for the companies. In the free trade system in effect in nearly all of Latin America, this would mean greater exports of capital to the United States — so, in short, the Alliance for Progress would become a means for Latin American countries to finance foreign monopolies.

Moreover, since the document contains no explicit decision on basic points, such as the maintenance of the prices of raw materials, an obligation to maintain those prices or a prohibition on lowering them, it is very probable that, in the coming years, the present trend will continue, and the prices of Latin America's raw materials will keep falling.

In that case, it is probable there will be an ever worsening deterioration in the balance of payments of each of the Latin American countries, to which will be added the effects of the export of capital by the monopolies. All this will translate into a lack of development—the opposite of what the Alliance for Progress is supposed to achieve. The lack of development will bring about more unemployment; unemployment will mean a real drop in wages; and an inflationary process—with which we are all familiar—will begin, in order to meet the shortages in the national budgets that are caused by lack of income. At that point, the International Monetary Fund will begin to play a preponderant role in nearly all the countries of Latin America.

That is when the crucial choice for the Latin American countries will arise. There are only two possible paths: to confront the people's discontent, with all that that entails, or to take the path of the liberation of foreign trade, which is of fundamental importance for our economies; to develop an independent economic policy; and to promote the development of all the domestic forces in the country—all this, naturally, within the framework of independent foreign policies that will lead to developing trade with countries in other parts of the world.

Naturally, not all countries will be able to do this, because it requires some special conditions. First of all, you need a lot of courage. Within the present system, the rulers will have to effect a great change in their economic and foreign policies and will immediately enter into conflict with the foreign monopolies. The masses will support the governments that enter into conflict to defend their citizens' standard of living, but, when the masses defend a position, they also make demands. So, the governments will be faced with a double threat, which they will not always manage to deal with successfully: pressure by the imperialist monopolies on the one hand and pressure by the masses, who will be demanding more, on the other. To really take such a road, you must break down former structures, place yourself on the side of the masses and initiate a thorough revolution. But we are not talking about revolution; we are talking about the path that the governments may follow without its leading to the outbreak of revolutionary processes.

Faced with this choice, if the rulers have the courage to confront the situation, if they satisfy a considerable part of the aspirations of the masses and if they do not back down under pressure from the foreign monopolies, they will be able to make progress for some time.

Unfortunately, what history shows us is that, when faced with this choice, the rulers, fearing pressure from the masses, ally themselves with the monopolies and the importing sector of the national bourgeoisie and initiate a stage of repression.

If an independent policy is to succeed, the government must have not only a strong, aggressive national bourgeoisie that wants improvement and is aware of its ideals but also an army that understands the present situation in Latin America and the rest of the world. We cannot predict whether or not this will happen.

The other path is that of the people's discontent. In these conditions, their discontent increases to the point that, once again, two historic alternatives arise and a choice has to be made: either the governments are replaced through elections and new governments are installed, this time with the masses' direct participation in power, or a state of civil war is established. If a government with participation by the masses comes to power, great contradictions will again arise between the masses, who will be trying to have their demands met, and the national armies, which defend different social strata and will still have the weapons. This is fertile ground for another civil war.

If the governments manage to eliminate the mass movement and maintain an iron grip on the government apparatus, the threat of civil war—for which Cuba states here and now it will not be responsible—will always hang over their heads. Those civil wars, which will begin in very difficult conditions, in the harshest terrain, will gradually spread to the countryside, laying siege to the cities, and one day the masses will seize political power.

Mr. President and fellow delegates, this is the message Cuba feels bound to convey to all of you: what it thinks about the Alliance for Progress, the dangers to be seen in the Alliance for Progress, and what it foresees in the future of the peoples, if— as has been the case so far—all international meetings turn into mere oratorical contests.

Therefore, while expressing its affinity with many of the aspirations set forth in this Punta del Este accord, Cuba regrets that it cannot sign it now; Cuba reiterates its desire for friendship with the peoples of the continent. It is willing to discuss any bilateral problem that may arise with other Latin American countries, and expresses its gratitude for the spirit of cooperation with which all delegates have listened to the comments by the Cuban delegation—its address, its warnings and its perhaps too-often-repeated and exhaustive explanations.

Thank you.

The Battle is Not Yet Decided

Press Conference in Cuba on the Punta del Este Conference
(August 23, 1961)

A televised press conference on August 23, 1961, discussing the recent Inter-American Economic and Social Council (CIES) in Punta del Este.

Moderator: Good evening, ladies and gentlemen. As you have heard, Dr. Ernesto Guevara, minister of the economy of the revolutionary government, is here with us tonight to report to the people of Cuba about the Punta del Este conference. The way he represented Cuba in that conference, in which insidious attempts were made to organize the other Latin American countries against Cuba, won him the respect of everyone — including our adversaries — and, naturally, the gratitude of all Cubans.

As you know, Dr. Guevara visited Buenos Aires at the conclusion of the Punta del Este conference and met with President Frondizi. After that, he went to Brasilia, where President Quadros presented him with the Order of the Southern Cross, Brazil's highest decoration. All this has increased the interest in his appearance tonight.

Dr. Guevara will begin by addressing you, after which, as usual, journalists may ask questions.

Che Guevara: Before answering the *compañero* journalists' questions, I will summarize — as briefly as possible — the results of the conference, its initial goals and the role that Cuba and the other countries played in it.

I will begin by explaining what the Inter-American Economic and Social Council (CIES) conference was. The CIES is a part of the Organization of American States (OAS) that concerns itself with economic matters in the Americas. Traditionally, it has been dominated by US imperialist interests, and has been completely under that influence up to now.

The Conference of Economic Ministers — and this is the source of the small mistake that [moderator] *compañero* [Luis Gómez] Wangüemert made, because I am not minister of the economy, though the conference was one of economic ministers — was held in order to establish an "Alliance for Progress," as Kennedy announced, and, naturally, to chain the Latin American countries more tightly to the financial organizations of Wall Street; to isolate Cuba; and, if possible, to organize another armed attack on Cuba.

We had some very important — and rather different — tasks: to work with our sister Latin American republics, to try to get the conference to adopt positions that were more in line with the peoples' interests, to unmask imperialism, and to counter its attempts to isolate us by isolating it instead. These were enormous goals, and it was not possible to achieve them in full, but we did manage to bring out some aspects that were important to the Latin American governments and peoples.

First of all, the falsehood of the Alliance for Progress was proved to the governments represented at the conference, along with the imperialist motives that lie behind it, in all the work, in all the little committees that were formed outside the conference. The North Americans' attempts to isolate us were exposed, and it was also made clear that the peoples and governments could not make progress along the path of humiliation and subjugation to the interests of Wall Street. Presumably, the countries that have shown a more independent attitude are those that have benefited the most from this Alliance for Progress, although, naturally, it is impossible to know what the exact results of the Alliance for Progress are as yet, for it is based on a framework of suppositions and lies that, in the best of cases, should still be judged by reality, and it is very probable that reality will show that it is an enormous confidence trick mounted against the Latin American peoples.

Right from the beginning of the conference, we described it as a political meeting and exposed the attempts being made to isolate Cuba. We strongly opposed the fifth point that was discussed in the fourth commission of the conference, related to promoting the Alliance for Progress plan. It was a plan for taming Latin American public opinion and placing it at the service of the United States. As soon as nearly all the large Latin American countries, headed by Brazil, Argentina, and Mexico, opposed that point — and many other, smaller nations, too — it was eliminated. Cuba led the discussion on this subject, and with good reason, as it was expressly named in the preliminary report — the document that was later called the preliminary report — which described Cuba as "a dictatorship that had eliminated all organs of the press."

The worst thing was not this political characterization of Cuba, but the fact that a supposed inter-American organization, in which all countries have the same rights, was allowing itself to judge and denounce Cuba's position, through the officials of that organization, who were also the owners of reactionary

Latin American newspapers. Thus, we were automatically denounced by an intercontinental organization, judged by a group of so-called experts, but without any trial by the Latin American nations.

Right from the start, the criticism of Cuba centered on that fifth point, which, as I have said, was eliminated, and it was replaced with a version which, though still poisonous, was much harder to pin down.

Naturally, different countries had very different positions. At the beginning, some formal mistakes were made that forced Cuba to protest. Minister of the Economy Beltrán Espantoso, the delegate from Peru, was named to represent all the visiting delegations in thanking President Haedo. It was a ceremonial role, and it should have been nothing more than a courteous address; but the Peruvian minister expressed a political opinion of the Alliance for Progress, placing it directly within the "Christian, Western civilization" of "representative democracy," with "free elections," etc. So Cuba had to protest. It was a double protest: first, because, in a ceremonial address, when you are representing all the countries, you should not express political opinions, which must be discussed; and, second, because Cuba had not been consulted on this and, without its agreement, the delegate from a country that did not have diplomatic relations with us had been named to represent all the countries.

At first, the situation was volatile, but the delegate from Ecuador immediately supported us, because he had not been consulted, either. Thus, some issues like this were brought out.

In the plenary session, before the various delegations took the floor, we expressed our thanks to the people and government of Uruguay and said that we were doing this independently because we did not agree with the statements that Mr. Beltrán had made earlier.

Several different positions were defined right from the start. Cuba's position, naturally, placed it at one extreme of the intercontinental struggle that was waged at Punta del Este. The United States was at the other extreme, and there was a very wide range in between that can be reduced to two or three main positions.

Most of the small Caribbean countries—and some South American countries, as well—took a servile position on the side of the United States, voting for all the measures that the United States proposed or that it proposed through other countries (usually Guatemala or Peru, though at times it also used others). The use of proxies is a common US tactic.

Some countries fought for specific economic measures, supposing that this was not a political conference; in other words, they did not take part in the political debates of the conference. These countries included Argentina and, to some extent, Mexico.

Other countries clearly recognized the importance of the need for Latin American unity, saw the danger of Cuba's isolation, and understood the basis of this Alliance for Progress. Their champion was Brazil, whose decisive action kept the conference from adopting other kinds of resolutions that could have been detrimental to the Cuban delegation. The specific instructions of President Quadros meant that, at all times, the United States had to restrain itself concerning Cuba, in order to avoid Brazil's voting against them.

Naturally, all of these are suppositions, because the discussions on the important issues at the conference did not take place publicly, but were held between delegations, and the

Cuban delegation never took part in them. We found out later through friends, journalists, or members of an enemy country's delegation who were personal friends and passed on the information. In other words, we found ourselves in the midst of a "cold war," and methods appropriate to a war were employed.

In addition, some countries—mainly Bolivia and Ecuador—took outstanding positions in the defense of democratic principles and the people's self-determination. They joined Cuba many times and showed the real importance that their governments gave to the conference. Because of them, Cuba never felt alone.

Bolivia's attitude was especially admirable and courageous in the conference—so much so that the members of cliques called its delegates "the Cubans' first cousins," a nickname that was very dangerous for a country in Bolivia's particular situation. The Bolivians' position on many points in the discussion was very outspoken.

The 10 or 12 days of discussions were very intense; we had to be constantly on guard in one commission or another—there were four commissions in total—and we had to fight against the attempts that were made to inject poison in the declarations, articles, and foundations of declarations in order to place Cuba in a difficult position.

In the general assembly, the Cuban delegation acted with great firmness; all of my *compañeros* did a tremendous job. We can say that the Cuban delegation was a model of discipline and that none of its members did anything at Punta del Este but work in the commissions in circumstances in which, as always happens in this kind of conference, some of the representatives of other countries hardly ever showed up but rather spent their time in the casinos and other such places of amusement, which were plentiful.

Naturally, with all the responsibilities it bears right now, Cuba could not allow itself to engage in that kind of thing, and its continuous work in all the commissions gradually modified even the approach of some countries that are out-and-out enemies of ours.

Cuba raised its voice, expressing its opinion, in all the commissions. Cuba's opinions were defeated in the votes, but many delegates who voted against them did so unwillingly.

When a foreign delegate greeted us publicly, it was a significant expression of independence and daring, because they then became the focus of all the other delegates' gaze, the cameras of the many representatives of the international press and the attention of the intelligence services — especially those of the United States.

Even so, there were many surprises. Many people approached us individually, saying that, in general, a new stage in the Americas had been initiated at Punta del Este. This new stage was created by the peoples' — or, rather, the governments' — sense of independence. Most of the peoples were not represented at Punta del Este — only the Cuban people and a few others. In general, the governments represented the oligarchies of each country, each one faced with serious problems, which made them realize it would be difficult to survive in the coming years. It is not a long-term problem any more, it is a problem of how to get through the coming months or the coming year, how to manage to hang on until the end of your term in office, how to manage to stay in power without causing upsets, without having to confront serious problems.

They had seen how Cuba's stance, two and a half years after

we had liberated ourselves, had increasingly become a head-on confrontation with the United States, but also seen that no catastrophe had occurred and that Cuba's development was very accelerated — which did not interest most of the countries very much, but they were interested in the fact that there were great possibilities for surviving, even against the will of the United States. This interested them because they used Cuba as a kind of blackmail. Sitting near us was a delegate of one of the dictatorial countries that has broken off relations with us — personally, he is a very nice man — and he admitted cynically that he was "in the beneficial shadow of Che, trying to see what I can get." Naturally, the "shadow of Che" was not the shadow of Che at all; it was the shadow of the Cuban revolution, which, with its steadfast attitude and complete denunciation all the North Americans' plans, enabled other countries to reap small benefits, and many of them did try to get something. For the first time in a Latin American conference, divergent voices were raised, which forced the United States change its strategy — a strategy it had been preparing for some time, with trips by the foreign ministers of other countries, statements by top-ranking US authorities aimed at creating a climate for holding a foreign ministers' conference to first call on Cuba to rejoin the Latin American countries, and abandon its "nefarious alliance" and then to denounce and isolate it.

The Punta del Este conference was a kind of advance payment made to the governments for their complicity in this. Even so, our attitude of resolute denunciation — as well as the support of Brazil, a country of enormous importance, and several other Latin American countries, categorically opposing the linking of this conference with any other one — seem to have put paid to US plans right now. I say "seem to have" because there is no way of knowing for sure what will happen. The United States is a very powerful country; it has a lot of levers for manipulating the oligarchies of the countries it controls, and it will keep on working in that regard. Nevertheless, we think that it will be very difficult for it to call a foreign ministers' conference right now.

It is hardly necessary to say that, if it does call such a conference and if it denounces us, it will not be anything more than a formal denunciation that the people will not support and that will be totally against themselves, and it will bring the countries that participate in it nothing but trouble. In any case, it will be very difficult to hold such a conference. Some of the very large countries, such as Brazil, have assured us that they will not participate in it; the president of Argentina adopted a similar stand yesterday; and Mexico's position on this is well known, so the most important Latin American countries are absolutely opposed to bringing any kind of political pressure to bear against Cuba.

The final result of the conference was a voluminous legacy setting forth the Latin American peoples' aspirations for the coming 10 years, in the decade of "accelerated, fruitful, democratic progress." It has a preamble, called the Declaration to the Peoples of the Americas, which tries to sum up the proceedings; it is a verbose summary, full of adjectives and no figures, but says nothing and makes nothing obligatory.

From the political point of view, the conference may be considered a resounding failure for US aspirations to denounce Cuba. From the viewpoint of its special economic policy, I doubt that it was such a great failure, because the United States has made the peoples — in other words, the governments, and, through the Latin American governments, the peoples —

believe that it is really willing to help them, when this is not the case at all. Even if it were willing to help, it cannot do so; and, even if it could, it would have to help the ruling circles allied to the monopoly interests in each country, not the ruling circles alone, so the investments would turn into new business for the monopolies or for the oligarchies themselves that want to deposit their money in the United States.

In other words, the wheel would come full circle—just as it used to do in Cuba, before liberation, when local groups joined forces with US interests, had common businesses favored by the government, made money, turned their money into dollars and deposited those dollars in the United States.

Naturally, that system in no way benefited the peoples. But the main statement, the main part of that long document called the Punta del Este accord is really the part in which the United States set the amounts it would give to Latin America. The paragraph where those amounts are set forth does not commit the United States, because it is drawn up so vaguely that, really, the United States can refer to this document to show that it has no basic obligations:

> The United States declares that, if the peoples of Latin America adjust their economic policies, the United States and other western powers, such as West Germany and Japan, might consider investing no less than US$20 billion over the course of the next decade.

In other words, it is filled with dubious phrases and, unquestionably, the United States does not pledge to do anything more than take some steps, look on with sympathy, and consider the possibilities. The only effective obligation of the United States is to give a billion dollars during this first year, but a billion dollars in such a way that half a billion has already been appropriated: that was the first half billion dollars that Congress had authorized; as for the other half million, we will have to see. Moreover, there was a requirement that complete projects would have to be submitted within 60 days of the signing of the Punta del Este accord.

It is impossible to present a project, or even a draft, in 60 days, so the only thing it will finance will be what has already been done, what has already been discussed. Some projects will be carried out in the northeastern part of Brazil with financing that has already been granted by the US government; presumably, there will be something in Argentina, too; there has been talk of building a hydroelectric power station in the Chocón region and irrigating the land. But the small countries will not be able to implement any kind of project, and they will see very little — if any — of that first billion dollars.

About that first $1 billion: half a billion is apparently real, and the other half billion is more a subject for discussion than anything else. As for the other $19 billion, it constitutes the nub of the confidence trick.

Therefore, in spite of everything, I feel the United States is still to impose a scheme of this kind, in spite of the new influences that have arisen, the new manifestations by the peoples. In reality, it is scandalous how the peoples are being swindled.

The US Senate and House of Representatives have the power to grant or withhold those loans. Therefore, Representative Dillon, the treasury secretary, simply came and made statements on his own behalf that now have to be ratified by Congress. And, as far as I can see, only cut-down versions of these commitments will be ratified, if any at all.

So, it is possible that none of the paltry offerings in the

declaration, considered to be cause for such great hope for the peoples, will materialize.

Even so, Cuba presented 29 projects, and the spirit of those projects—none of which were approved in full—is reflected in some of the document's resolutions. Even the United States signed the document, but it lodged two formal reservations on chapter 3, which concerns raw materials and is a fundamental issue. Point 1 in that chapter was about development planning, which later became development programming—the name was changed. Point 2 concerned the integration of a Latin American common market. Point 3 was about raw materials and problems related to their prices and markets. Point 4 was the annual report to be prepared, with participation by economic ministers, in a different country in the Americas each year. Point 5, about making the Alliance for Progress better known, was practically eliminated. In its present form, point 5 is of no interest; point 4 is merely administrative, about the annual report; so the discussion centered around the other three points.

Not much importance was given to Latin American economic integration, and the United States waged its battle in commissions 1 and 3.

Commission 3, where *compañero* Raúl León Torras, Cuban undersecretary of trade dedicated a great deal of time and effort, was where the Latin American governments attained the best positions and where the United States lodged two formal reservations. The United States practically dominated the situation on point 1 and established a general program that did not really have any important content for the peoples.

The conference was important because it has reduced the possibility that a foreign ministers' conference will be held in the near future; and eliminated the possibility of isolating Cuba. It is now possible for Cuba's voice to be heard all over Latin America, in spite of enormous difficulties such as the frequent distortions of Cuba's comments by the Uruguayan newspapers as well as the newspapers of other countries. Nevertheless, it was still possible to tell the people the truth.

The conference was also important because a new language was spoken there—not just that of Cuba, which spoke forthrightly, in the language of open rebelliousness, but also the language of those countries that are not willing to be dumb beasts serving the United States and that argued to obtain better treatment for the products made from their raw materials.

More than anything, it was important because of the new stance of the Brazilian government—or, rather, the position taken by the new Brazilian government, because the position is not new. Ever since President Quadros took office, he has spoken out in no uncertain terms in favor of the coexistence of all peoples on earth, relations with all peoples, and a policy of peace.

I place considerable importance on the resolution that was adopted by a majority vote, which explicitly establishes the right of countries with different social systems to coexist in Latin America. It states—just a second, so I can read the exact words. It says:

> The active participation of the private sector is of basic importance to the desired process of economic development and integration, and, except in those countries where the free enterprise system does not exist, the programming of development by the appropriate national public bodies, far from hindering that participation, may facilitate and channel it, opening up new social benefits.

The original version did not contain the words "except in those countries where the free enterprise system does not exist," which were proposed by Cuba. This was because in speaking of the active participation of the private sector, it was a contradiction in the case of Cuba, as the exploitation of human by human and the philosophy of free enterprise have been condemned here.

The countries in commission 2 approved it by a simple major- ity — which was possible — of nine votes, after which it went to the plenary, where it was again approved, though with some variations — the original text was somewhat different. It was approved there by 11 votes — in other words, by the absolute majority, because there were 21 participating countries, and an absolute majority (11) was required — over the negative vote of the United States. Thus, the fact that countries that do not have a free-enterprise regime can belong to the inter-American system was inserted into the final documents of the Punta del Este accord, or, rather, of the Latin American conference.

We proclaimed this as one of the achievements of the confer- ence, and it provoked a violent, angry, inopportune reaction by [US] Treasury Secretary Dillon, who announced that he did not recognize Cuba and did not recognize peaceful coexistence — in short, that he was going to chew us up into little pieces that day or the next.

Those are the positive aspects of the conference, things that are unquestionably very important. The negative aspects are, as I have already told you, the fact that, once more, the United States spread the false idea that it is spending money to help the peoples. No such thing. First of all, it is not spending money, and, next, if it should spend any, it will not be to help the peoples; if it spends anything, it would be to help its own monopolies, which will return the money, sending it back to the United States.

So, as they say, "dust to dust," and the dollars—at least the ones in Latin America—will keep going back to the United States. So, if those dollars are spent—which is a very big if, as it is much more probable that Congress will not even appropriate them—they will be for the monopolies in general, which, after using the money and making new profits, will send it back to the United States. That is a negative thing, and so is the poverty of the aspirations contained in this document.

In the field of education, Cuba has achieved practically everything that is proposed for the next 10 years, and it will achieve some of the things that it has not yet achieved and surpass those goals within five years.

We think that the per capita net rate of development of 2.5 percent is very low; we aspire to a rate of at least 10 percent. We had done some calculations—which Mr. Dillon did not like, either—and they showed that, if all the countries of Latin American had a growth rate of 2.5 percent and, based on it, tried to reach the standard of living the United States has now, it would take us 100 years to do so. And, if we tried to reach the standard of living the United States would have by then—because it would be growing, too, even though slowly—it would take us 500 years to do so. So, the "tremendous Alliance for Progress" means that only several generations later will our descendants be able to consider themselves to be on a par with the United States. What our peoples want is a growth rate that will free them from poverty now, not think about how to go about it and keep getting put off, which is the plan of the United States.

The health plan is very limited, too, and it even makes some specifications we consider negative. It says that 70 percent of the houses will have water within 10 years. In other words, it is explicitly condemning 30 percent of the houses in Latin America's urban areas not to have running water or sewerage services, etc. In the countryside, 50 percent of the houses will not have these services.

The plan for housing construction was not approved. The only country that presented a draft in this regard was Cuba, supported by Brazil. The United States objected to it, however, and, in the end, the Cuban motion was rejected. Thus, the Alliance for Progress contains no specific plan for providing houses for the people. We had done some calculations which showed that it would cost around 2 billion pesos a year just to meet the housing deficit that will be created in the coming years. So the Alliance for Progress funds would be completely used just to fulfill the housing need.

The conference's housing plan began with a very wordy invocation; it spoke of a decade of vigorous democratic growth and of the achievements that the peoples would attain within the system of "representative democracy." It said that Latin America had been and was an example of freedom for all the peoples, and so on. And then it said that 70 percent of the houses in the urban areas and 50 percent of the ones in the countryside would have water and that we would equal the development of the United States in around 500 years, or attain its present development in 100 years. It said all this, but, naturally, in such a way that those who do not understand a few of these things — which is normal among the people — would not see it.

Moreover, the only document that was presented — apart from Cuba's — was one that does not contain any figures. Thus, everything was reduced to formulations such as:

> To promote, within the specific characteristics of each country, programs of integral agrarian reform aimed at the effective transformation, where this is required, of the structures to a fair system of land ownership and exploitation, with a view to replacing the system of large and small landholdings with a fair system of ownership.

This is nothing more than an empty exhortation because "within the specific characteristics of each country and where this is required" means that nobody will carry out an agrarian reform.

It says that the countries should "develop programs of health and hygiene, with a view to preventing disease, fighting against epidemics and, in short, defending the human potential." This means nothing concrete. If anything, what this reference to "human potential" means is that the work force needed by the monopolies, in order to have people work for them, has to be defended.

It continues:

> To ensure that the workers receive fair remuneration and adequate working conditions; to establish efficient systems of worker-employer relations and procedures of consultation and cooperation between the authorities of the employers' associations and the workers' organizations, to promote socioeconomic development; to put an end to illiteracy — *this is the only concrete thing* — extend, in the shortest possible time, the benefits of elementary or primary education to all Latin Americans; and vastly expand the opportunities of secondary, technical, and higher education.

In other words, it is a very broad plan, with a lot of very pretty words, but it does not force anybody to do anything and does not explain anything. This is what the Latin American peoples will know as the result of two weeks' deliberations at Punta del Este.

There is only one phrase in this last document that may commit the United States. It continues as follows:

> The United States, for its part, pledges to offer its financial and technical cooperation to achieve the goals of the Alliance for Progress.
>
> For that purpose, it will provide most of the financing of at least US$20 billion, mainly in public funds, that Latin America needs from all external sources during the next decade to complement its own efforts.

In other words, it pledges to provide most of the financing — at least US$20 billion — but Congress probably will not appropriate the money; or, if it does agree to the loans, they will not ever arrive.

And then it says,

> In the 12 months from March 13, 1961, date of the first declaration of the Alliance for Progress, the United States will provide over a billion dollars in public funds to contribute immediately to Latin America's economic and social progress.
>
> The United States intends that the loans for development will be long-term, and, when appropriate, they will be extended for up to 50 years, at a generally low rate of interest or without interest, as the case may be.

So the vagueness continues. This is the net result, my view of the pros and cons of the CIES conference. The balance sheet was positive for Cuba, but negative in the economic sphere because the United States once again pulled the wool over the peoples' eyes and, with the help of the corrupt press of all the countries, has made the people in some places believe that this Alliance offers some hope.

In general, in private talks, the delegates expressed the opinion that this was just one more meeting like so many others, and many of them were very philosophical about it.

As I said, they went to play roulette at the casino and go to parties; sometimes the chairs were empty, because all the members of a delegation had left and had no interest in the outcomes, because they knew that the results were more or less pre-determined and that the small countries with puppet governments could do nothing to change those results. So, they adopted a more practical approach and sometimes did not even attend.

I think that I've talked enough, and the journalists should have a chance.

Moderator: *Compañero* Honorio Muñoz, would you like to ask the first question?

Journalist: Yes. Commander Guevara, even though the Cuban delegation's viewpoints and achievements at the Punta del Este conference were publicized in Cuba and you have just given us a clear and exhaustive critical appraisal of the conference, I believe that some points of Cuba's position, of its political focus, should be further clarified.

For example, in the conference you said, "The 'Alliance for Progress' is conceived within the imperialist framework, in order to save it." Why do you think this?

Che Guevara: This is an important point. Naturally, the United States has changed its system—but only formally, because the imperialist system cannot really change. What has changed is its system of relations with the Latin American countries. It has become aware of one fundamental thing, which is that the colonial system, even when it is the economic colonialism from which the Latin American peoples suffer, is in such a process of disintegration that it cannot last. The vestiges of feudalism have to disintegrate quickly.

The United States has drawn up a plan for ending the feudal relations of production—above all, in the countryside, where most of the Latin American countries have fundamental problems—and for carrying out a kind of agrarian reform. As it says, it will put an end to large and small landholdings—in other words, it will support the creation of medium-sized, mechanized landholdings, using agricultural workers instead of small farmers. This will promote greater productivity, which will make it possible to dump large quantities of products on the market, wipe out the parasitical feudal class, and create a new class—no, probably not a new class, but a particular kind of bourgeoisie, linked to imports in each Latin American country, which will establish relations with the US monopolies and create mixed companies.

Those mixed companies will function under the system established in each country, except for their profits, which will be under the free exchange system and can be exported to the United States. Thus, everything that is volatile, such as the direct intervention of foreign capital in a country's economy, will be hidden. As happened here in Cuba, they will be called the "Cuban Electric Company," the "Colombian Telephone Company," the "Peruvian Iron Company," etc., and they will have an administrator in the host country, the country where the raw material is, but the capital and financial control will be in US hands.

So, as I have already said, the United States will develop the country's production, do away with feudalism, create this new class and then initiate a stage of capitalist development in all of those countries — development that will, however, be distorted because the capital invested will not be independent. It will be the capital of the national bourgeoisie which has some conflict of interest with the monopolies, but is, nevertheless, tied to monopoly capital. It will therefore continue to contribute to the country's colonization, alleviate a little pressure, and, naturally, provide a modest boost, along with the short-term investment measures in the economies of the most backward countries, where the danger of a social explosion is most evident.

This is happening, for example — and this is no secret — in Haiti, the Dominican Republic, nearly all the Central American and the Andean countries, where there is still large-scale feudalism. Estates are still sold in Peru "with all their workers." In other words, the workers are considered to be a part of the estate's value. Thus, a lot of work can still be done within the capitalist system to put an end to the most backward relations of production and still keep them within the imperialist system.

Moreover, all the manual labor that still exists in those countries can be eliminated. This is not a new experience. It was first employed by England, in its colonization of India, many years ago, when the introduction of English capital wiped out the feudal relations of production in many regions — eliminated the feudal relations of production so that India would become a great exporter of raw materials to England.

The United States is trying to perfect the English system and turn Latin America into an efficient producer of raw materials for the United States, doing away with the points of greatest conflict in the relations of production, such as — in nearly all of the countries — the relations between the small farmers and the feudal lords.

I do not know if I've explained this clearly.

Moderator: *Compañero* Ithiel León.

Journalist: Commander Guevara, I would like you to expand a little on the previous question, because it has been said that, all things considered, the Alliance for Progress will bring about greater unemployment, a drop in wages and inflation in the countries in which it operates.

Che Guevara: Well, it is not exactly the Alliance for Progress but the process that will bring about that outcome. I described this as the process that Latin America would follow — and that it will follow in any case, with or without the Alliance for Progress.

To be precise, I said that the Alliance for Progress was not going to result in any significant amount of capital for Latin America and that, even if it were to do so, the capital would be provided with conditions set by imperialism, and the investments would be channeled toward those places where monopoly capital wanted it to go.

In other words, to all the extracting companies in Latin America that are going to produce minerals — strategic raw materials for the United States — the producers of raw materials are also going to produce other raw materials (for example, agricultural ones) that are important for the United States.

If investments are made under the Alliance for Progress, all they will do is bring about a minor upsurge in business, and that upsurge will only mean greater profits for those companies, which will re-export them to the United States, and then we will be back at square one, right? But the process continues; the increase in production when there is no real increase in markets—the capitalist market is not in a stage of expansion right now—means that there is more pressure weighing on trade and the producers are forced to increase productivity in order to lower the cost of the product.

An increase in productivity in the capitalist system automatically means unemployment. Unemployment, when there are no alternative jobs, means a lowering of real wages. Moreover, as in the struggles that ensue when several countries produce the same raw material, there is an effective decrease in the amount of money received, which also means a shortage of imports, and the shortage of imports results in higher prices— an increase in the cost of living. All together, the increase in the cost of living, unemployment, and the lowering of real wages caused by the number of people who are unemployed creates hunger and a chain of bankruptcies and losses because of the decrease in the market—all those people who have stopped consuming. And, naturally, this brings about a drop in the amount of taxes collected, an imbalance between the amount of taxes the governments receive and their liabilities, which gives rise to inflation and leads to the total deterioration of the economy.

At that moment, I said, the International Monetary Fund (IMF), to which all Latin American countries belong, would intervene to take monetary or anti-infringement monetary measures. Those measures would mean a further curtailment of credit in order to try to reduce inflation by cutting back on the amount of money in circulation instead of reducing inflation by increasing production. In order to increase production, it would be necessary to do away with the existing relations of production, to do away with the present relations of agricultural production and have the people take over the factories—in short, carry out a real social revolution.

Since it is impossible that the IMF will decide on or advise this, the situation will deteriorate, and I pointed out that countries would have only two choices—or, rather, would have to choose between two alternatives.

They can diversify their foreign trade, adopting a new policy of selling to the rest of the world—which was the basis of our own development, in contrast with trading mainly with the United States. This will bring about a series of contradictions that are already known: the monopolies will become aggressive; the country will have to take new measures; it will become necessary to depend ever more on the people; and, as is only logical, the people, too, will demand more. The position held by the bourgeoisie will challenged, and this may lead to a social revolution—or, in any case, to a situation in which the national bourgeoisie is in constant conflict with monopoly capital.

The other alternative is to confront the people's discontent, to follow the directives of the IMF and other such agencies, to control the people's exasperation with drastic measures and to initiate a stage of very serious civil strife. An administration facing this situation will be voted out of office, the new administration that replaces it will renew the struggle to diversify trade, and the struggle with the people will begin again. This was explained succinctly and well in the script of one of Sartre's movies some years ago, called "L'Engranage."

This process of administrations being voted in and out is always permeated with fear of making the definitive decision, which is that of taking over the means of production and handing them over to the people, as was done in Cuba, which has enabled us to take a big step toward socialist revolution.

That was what I said in my final address at Punta del Este.

Moderator: *Compañero* Gregorio Ortega.

Journalist: After the Punta del Este conference, Commander Guevara, you went to Brazil. What can you tell us about your meeting with Janio Quadros?

Che Guevara: It was a very short meeting. President Quadros paid me several honors. The first was that of waiting to chat with me for a few moments, because he had already promised to inaugurate an iron and steel plant in one of the states in Brazil, so it could not be a very long talk.

Quadros has already talked about the results of that conversation, in which he simply reaffirmed Brazil's position of resolute support for Cuba, of support for the people's self-determination. We talked a little about the economic mission that is in Cuba right now and about the Brazilian government's decision to come to a rapid agreement on initiating new aspects of trade with us. And, in a demonstration of affection for our government—not for me personally, but for the Cuban government—the highest Brazilian decoration was bestowed on me. This sums up my talk with President Quadros.

Moderator: *Compañero* Honorio Muñoz.

Journalist: Without departing from the Punta del Este conference, what can you tell us about one of the peripheral episodes that is least known here and which UPI reported on, if not today, then recently. UPI says, and other journalists—South Americans, I think—also state that, on one occasion, you met with a Mr. Goodwin, who, I think, is a personal delegate of Mr. Kennedy. What can you tell us about this? Did that meeting take place, or not? And, in general, what can you tell us about it?

Che Guevara: It is true that I met with Mr. Goodwin, but he was not really Kennedy's envoy. He is one of Kennedy's advisers and he was at the Punta del Este conference.

Some Brazilian friends invited me to a small, intimate get-together, and Mr. Goodwin was there. As some of the agencies reported, we talked, chatting on personal subjects. We were both the guests of a third person, a Brazilian official, and we talked as private individuals, not as representatives of our governments. I was not authorized to have any kind of a talk with a US official, and he was not authorized to have one with me, so, within the limits of my English—which, as you have seen, is quite poor—and Mr. Goodwin's Spanish, which is nonexistent, we exchanged a few words with the help of a Brazilian official, who served as translator.

At one point, Mr. Goodwin said that he neither represented nor was authorized to speak in the name of his government but that he would convey some observations that Cuba made to his government. I limited myself to setting forth Cuba's publicly established position: that we are willing to talk; that we do not seek a quarrel of any kind but will take all the way to the end any quarrel that is forced on us; that we want to be part of the Latin American system; that we are united culturally with the rest of Latin America and want to remain so; and that we insist on our right to be treated like any other country in Latin America or in the Organization of American States, only with a different social and economic organization, and that our absolute right to have whatever friends we want, anywhere in the world, be respected.

In short, it was a brief, courteous, cool exchange, as might be expected of two functionaries of countries that are officially enemies, right? It was not seen as important until some journalist or functionary — perhaps of the Argentine embassy or government or a Brazilian journalist; I do not really know who — publicized it. That was all.

Moderator: *Compañero* Ithiel León.

Journalist: Commander, I have heard that the delegation representing Trujillo's son's regime [in the Dominican Republic] also signed the Alliance for Progress accord. Do you know what that country's situation is within the so-called inter-American system?

Che Guevara: Well, you know, it was not possible to speak about politics in the CIES conference. We did not have any relations with the Balaguer Administration, and the situation in Santo Domingo is very special. The delegates from the Dominican Republic did not say anything in the conference. They abstained from all discussion, though they always voted — naturally, the way the United States did. Sometimes their chief delegate was not there; I do not know where he was, but he was absent many times.

The government's attitude there was very correct, because it was totally alienated from the conference. There was never any talk of excluding the Dominican Republic from the Alliance for Progress. Naturally, there was not talk of excluding anybody. For example, we asked several times if Cuba would be included in the Alliance for Progress, if Cuba would be entitled to Alliance for Progress funds, and Mr. Dillon did not reply. Naturally, the chairperson of the assembly did not know; he had no reason for knowing—he was the delegate of another country who had been elected there—and he asked Mr. Dillon, but Mr. Dillon did not answer him, either. So, the question remained, like in a mystery story, up to the last day, when Dillon made a final brusque remark, saying that Cuba would not get anything from the Alliance for Progress. He then held a press conference in which he spoke about Cuba, naturally, but the journalists also asked him about Stroessner's regime, in Paraguay, and about the Dominican Republic. He gave an evasive reply but let it be known that the Dominican Republic would be included in the Alliance for Progress and would be one of the countries to benefit.

More or less tacitly, it is assumed that Trujillo's death has already lessened the guilt of the other members of the ruling team and that it can already be called democratic, because the father died, and all the others are very, very minor figures, and their punishments will be very, very short. So that situation remained hovering in the air, even though not a word was spoken there about the Dominican regime.

Moderator: *Compañero* Gregorio Ortega.

Journalist: How did the Uruguayan people express their solidarity with our revolution, commander?

Che Guevara: The Uruguayan people expressed their solidarity in practically every possible way. Their enthusiasm was really moving, and it caused a kind of upset in protocol and practice for us: the Cuban delegates were the only ones that the people—the few workers, because it was a typical beach resort—waited for to applaud and greet. It is important to note this: Punta del Este is a beach resort around 170 kilometers from Montevideo, the capital, and it has a harsh climate in the winter, the season it was when we were in the Southern Hemisphere, so there was nobody around—no workers, no other people. Therefore, except for a few isolated instances, it was impossible to experience the Uruguayan people's solidarity at Punta del Este.

But, when we arrived in Montevideo, it was tremendous. I had to give a talk on Cuban economic development in the assembly hall of the university, which was a rather small place. It was jam-packed. It had been attacked by groups of students—financed by the United States, of course—and, at midday, the university official had had to open the doors pistol in hand; then those students threw stink-bombs all over the assembly hall. I gave my talk in an atmosphere of chlorophyll room fresheners, but the people there were very enthusiastic— so much so that I had to ask them many times to restrain themselves, because I had promised the government that I would do everything possible to avoid incidents.

The people were also wonderfully disciplined and had a great spirit of cooperation, in addition to tremendous enthusiasm, which really made me feel I was in Cuba. But when I left—and how this happened is not clear—it seems that some-body fired on some of the cars or simply shot over the people's heads to provoke a reaction. So, the meeting, which had been filled with great enthusiasm and had been held in a perfectly normal way, was clouded by the death of a professor [Arbelio Ramírez] of the institute, who had come to hear me. He was shot in the neck and died a few minutes later. The people reacted to that violently, falling on the presumed attackers; the police intervened; and there was a kind of showdown between the police and the demonstrators.

I found out later that there were more incidents the next day, at the professor's funeral. In addition, the Government Council met and timidly denounced the episode, saying that it was not "diplomatic" — something to that effect—for a guest at the CIES conference to take part in a political meeting. Naturally, I had not taken part in a political meeting, because they had said it was to be a technical meeting, and a talk about economic development has to be technical. Of course, when it is Cuba's economic development that is being discussed, and when the conditions for economic development are such that the people assume the political direction of the government, take over the factories, carry out an agrarian reform, and, in passing, do away with the oppressor's army, as well, then, naturally, the basic theses of economic development turn into political theses. But we have always said that you cannot separate political and economic issues.

In addition, I had taken all the necessary precautions: I had spoken with the [Uruguayan] president and the minister of the interior and said that I wanted to attend the talk but left it to the government to make the decision, and they expressly authorized my participation.

On the afternoon before the conference, one of the members of the Government Council, who had been president of the university the preceding year, made a radio address to the army asking it to take charge of the situation—to prevent subversion and a coup d'état. When we left, the situation was very tense.

After all those events, the Uruguayan people went to the hotel where I was staying to express their affection in a thousand ways. There were so many representatives of groups that the owner of the hotel decided that delegations could not go upstairs, so there were some incidents. I could not speak with all of the delegations that came to see me, which would have been nearly impossible anyway, because there were so many of them. The people's enthusiasm was very great at all times.

Moderator: *Compañero* Honorio Muñoz.

Journalist: Che Guevara, at Punta del Este, you challenged imperialism to an emulation between its plan, called the Alliance for Progress, and what our country has achieved. Our country, which is carrying out a socialist revolution, has the support of the socialist world, good relations with many countries that are not socialist and the friendship of the peoples of the world. On what do you base your confidence that we will win that competition?

Che Guevara: On economics. That was a meeting in which they wanted to show everybody the possibilities of "representative democratic development," etc., and they were talking about a rate of development of 2.5 percent. That figure alone destroyed the challenge, because we had a tremendous advantage: for us, in Cuba's present conditions, 10 percent is a slow rate of development; 2.5 percent, in Latin America's conditions, is considered an optimal or close to optimal rate of development. So, our minimum was four times as great as their optimum. In terms of economic development, this is an immense difference.

Moreover, I was led to issue that challenge because of my certainty that planned development is the only way of effectively guaranteeing that every economic policy that is followed will be applied fully and that correct policies of economic planning can only be developed and development with high growth rates can only be achieved when the people have control over the means of production. As I have said, it is very easy to see what the final result or the results at any moment — in 10 years or right now — will be.

It is enough to examine the goals that were proposed in education; we have already reached them. For example, one of the paragraphs says,

> That the following be adopted as goals of the Alliance for Progress in the field of education, to be reached in the next 10 years:
>
> (a) at least six years of free, obligatory primary education for all children of school age.

We set ourselves a goal of nine years. In the first program, they had proposed four years. We proposed nine years, because this year we're beginning a system of nine years of free, obligatory education for the Cuban people.

> (b) The carrying out of systematic campaigns of adult education, promoting community development, job training, cultural development and the eradication of illiteracy.

This is vague and speaks of the eradication of illiteracy, which we have already achieved to a very large extent this year and will fully accomplish next year, when we wipe out the last few pockets of illiteracy. And this is a 10-year plan [of the Alliance for Progress]. We are already advancing rapidly in providing job training and cultural development.

> (c) The reform and extension of high school education, so that a much higher proportion of the new generation will have an opportunity to continue their general education.

We have proposed to extend high school education to all young people of school age and to reform education so much that we completely nationalize it and place all the country's means of education at the service of the people.

> (d) The preparation of studies to determine what skilled labor is required for the development of industry, agrarian reform, and agriculture; plans for social development and public administration at all levels; and the establishment of crash programs for training and follow-up programs for those personnel.

We have already done all this, so it is easy for us to see that, since they need 10 years to do what we have already done, Cuba is bound to win this contest.

And then it talks about "the reform, extension, and improvement of higher education, so that a much higher proportion of young people have access to it." In other words, there is a great lack of precision in the Alliance for Progress mandate, while we are already giving scholarships and are increasing the number of university students, quite substantially in the most important disciplines.

Some other proposals even include some Cuban proposals —
for example:

> (g) The intensification of exchanges among students, teachers,
> professors, researchers, and other specialists, in order to stimu-
> late mutual understanding and make the best possible use of
> the means of information and research.

This is based on a Cuban proposal, which was changed, of
course; our version was better documented and more precise
than this one, but at least it is here. Another says:

> The establishment of a system of scholarships and other forms
> of social and economic assistance for students in order to
> reduce the number of dropouts, especially in rural areas, and
> to ensure effective equal opportunity to education at all levels.

This, too, is based on a Cuban proposal for establishing full
scholarships — here, the delegates took out the word "complete,"
or "full" — which Cuba is also doing to a large extent.

The public health program and the housing program —
which does not even exist — clearly show that the Alliance for
Progress cannot compete at all with Cuba's development, not
in the economic sphere, and much less in the social sphere,
where Cuba's progress is even greater.

Moderator: *Compañero* Ithiel León.

Journalist: During your trip, commander, in addition to meeting with President Janio Quadros, you also met with another
head of state, President Arturo Frondizi of Argentina. What
can you tell us about this other meeting?

Che Guevara: As you know, my meeting with Frondizi was held in rather abnormal conditions. In cases of personal meetings, I let the head of state or host officials of the nation that has received our officials issue their account of the meeting. The meeting with President Frondizi was held behind closed doors, and I believe that President Frondizi is the one who is authorized, in this case, to make a statement and say what we talked about. He has already done so; he issued statements today referring in a laudatory, positive way to Cuba and especially to the people's self-determination—which is vital to us, because we do not expect the other Latin American peoples to defend our social system, but we do want them to defend our right to have the social system we choose, which is what President Frondizi has done.

In addition, I had another meeting, with another head of state, President Haedo. It was very cordial and took place in Uruguay; there is not any secret about it. President Haedo loves jokes, and we were in a jovial mood, swapping jokes and drinking maté, which is an old habit I haven't forgotten and which I rediscovered in Uruguay. It was really a very pleasant meeting, held just after the president met with Mr. Dillon, so the priority was the United States first and Cuba second.

Moderator: *Compañero* Gregorio Ortega.

Journalist: With our questions, commander, we have asked you to expand on the summary you gave of the Punta del Este conference. We do not know if we have left anything out. Would you like to make a statement summing up the results of the Punta del Este conference for Latin America—and for the Cuban people, of course?

Che Guevara: I think that, what with my summary and your questions, everything important has already been said, though some explanation of the final vote, the voting in the commission, may be lacking. I do not remember what its name was, but it was the main commission of the conference, to which the papers of the four working commissions were brought. They were divided into chapters.

When we abstained from voting on the first declaration, which was called the Declaration to the Peoples of the Americas—we did not vote against it, we abstained, and I have already read you some paragraphs of that declaration—we explained why we were abstaining. Then we also abstained on the Punta del Este accord, and then also on the attached resolutions, which were about socioeconomic development, economic integration (we voted for the section on economic integration), basic export products (on which we abstained), the Annual Assessment of Socioeconomic Progress (which we voted for), and Public Opinion and the Alliance for Progress (which we voted against). This last is the title to which the original US paper was reduced. Though whittled down, it was still encumbered with a range of matters that were useless for an economic conference and bearing a considerable load of poison for the peoples of Latin America, in the form of subsidies and the regimentation of culture.

At first, there was a reference to a "common market of culture," as if it were a great conquest of Latin America; that phrase was used to describe point 5. The refutations were so harsh—and not only ours, but several other countries, as well— that this phrase was left out.

The only thing we voted for was the Annual Assessment of Socioeconomic Progress, because Cuba can check its progress in that assessment every year, and the results of the challenge can be seen. So, we will be there every year, showing what we have done and reminding the others that the document was signed and that a pledge was made to the peoples. That was the only thing we voted for. We abstained on all the others except the point on "Public Opinion and the Alliance for Progress," which we voted against.

I think that the main results of the conference are clear: what the United States proposed, what it got and what it did not get—and what it did not get is much more important than what it got. Then there was what Cuba proposed (I think it got nearly everything) and the phenomenon of the rise of other Latin American countries to an important plane in the political balance of forces of the Americas. This is particularly true of Brazil, whose decisions (perhaps for the first time in many years, or even for the first time in the history of "Pan-Americanism") now have to be taken into consideration in Washington and on Wall Street and cannot be ignored.

So, those are the final results of this episode in the struggle between the Latin American peoples and imperialism, the ministerial CIES conference at Punta del Este. It is a struggle that has not been decided in favor of anybody, but this episode may well have been a battle that Cuba—or, rather, the progressive forces in Latin America—won. It should be repeated in the struggles of Latin American countries at the ministerial level, in their struggles against imperialist aggression, against economic aggression and to guide the Latin American peoples. It should also be repeated in the daily reaffirmation of our aspirations to have the rest of Latin America share our future, with a fairer social system.

All this is to say that time will tell what the real results of the conference have been. It was a battle that may be just the first of a series of battles that imperialism will lose, or it may not be so important. It was held only a short time ago, and too short a time especially for those of us who participated, and who, therefore, have a rather distorted view of its problems—to be able to make an objective assessment.

But, yes, I believe the final results have been positive.

Moderator: Commander Guevara, *compañero* Honorio Muñoz would like to ask you one more question before this question period ends.

Journalist: Allow me a small follow-up, to ask what you think of the First National Production Assembly, that will begin in Havana on the 26th.

Che Guevara: The idea of calling that assembly arose only a few days ago, and I have been away. Now, I am getting back into the saddle at the ministry [of industry] again, and I have just learned about it as I have been working on my report to the people of Cuba.

If it is held in the way it should be, a production assembly would be very useful. In such an assembly, the main mistakes made in applying economic policy and the main personal mistakes made by the administrators of the various enterprises—enterprises and factories, right?—should be brought out, but in a spirit of constructive criticism. In other words, we should not—and it is good to warn about this—allow ourselves to get into personal arguments and accusations. It is an opportunity for airing and solving all the problems that exist— but on the basis of constructive criticism, not accusations.

We are not interested in showing that one specific individual or another has done a bad job. Rather, we want to focus on those areas in the economy where the work is not up to scratch and ensure that those problems are corrected. So, if a message prior to the meeting is worth anything, my advice to the *compañeros* is that they prepare for it in this way — that they go after the problems.

There's one more important thing: a good revolutionary should be familiar with whatever problems exist in the organizations they are in charge of. For the good functioning of that assembly, there should be criticism, of course; but the focus should be on self-criticism, not general criticism. In that spirit, we should all admit our own mistakes and try to find solutions for them by means of a harmonious discussion by representatives of all the productive forces in Cuba — with whom, I think, I'm going to meet at 9:00 on Saturday morning.

Moderator: And, now that Dr. Guevara has completed his report and clear explanation and answered the journalists' questions, I thank him and the Cuban people and bid our viewers good night.

NEW BOOKS FROM OCEAN PRESS

CHÁVEZ

Venezuela and the New Latin America

Hugo Chávez, interviewed by Aleida Guevara

Is Venezuela the new Cuba? Elected by overwhelming popular mandate in 1998, Hugo Chávez is now one of Latin America's most outspoken political figures. In this extraordinary interview with Che Guevara's daughter Aleida, Chávez expresses a fiercely nationalist vision for Venezuela and a commitment to a united Latin America.

ISBN 1-920888-00-4 (Also available in Spanish 1-920888-22-5)

CAPITALISM IN CRISIS

Globalization and World Politics Today

By Fidel Castro

Cuba's leader adds his voice to the growing international chorus against neo-liberalism and globalization. "Why not seek other formulas and admit that human-kind is able to organize itself in a more rational and humane manner?" asks Fidel Castro, denouncing a system that colonized, enslaved and plundered the peoples of the globe for centuries.

ISBN 1-876175-18-4

THE BOLIVIAN DIARY

Authorized Edition

Ernesto Che Guevara

Preface by Camilo Guevara, Introduction by Fidel Castro

This is Che Guevara's famous last diary, found in his backpack when he was captured by the Bolivian army in October 1967. It became an instant international best-seller. Newly revised, with a preface by Che's eldest son Camilo and extra-ordinary unpublished photos, this is the definitive, authorized edition of the diary, which after his death catapulted Che to iconic status throughout the world.

ISBN 1-920888-24-1 (Also available in Spanish ISBN 1-920888-30-6)

NEW BOOKS FROM OCEAN PRESS

CHE GUEVARA READER
Writings on Politics and Revolution

This new edition of the best-selling *Che Guevara Reader* features the most complete selection of Guevara's writings, letters, and speeches available in English. It includes essays on the Cuban revolutionary war and guerrilla warfare, his analysis of the first years of the Cuban revolution and his vision for Latin America and the Third World.

ISBN 1-876175-69-9 (Also available in Spanish ISBN 1-876175-93-1)

LATIN AMERICA
Awakening of a Continent
Ernesto Che Guevara

For many, the name Che Guevara is synonymous with Latin America. In fact, few individuals are so closely related to the history and struggles of their continent. This book presents Che's overall vision for Latin America: from his youthful travels until his death in Bolivia. Here, the reader can observe Che's development from spectator to participant in the struggles of Latin America, and finally to theoretician of the Latin American reality.

ISBN 1-920888-38-1 (Also available in Spanish ISBN 1-876175-71-0)

Centro de Estudios
CHE GUEVARA

oceanpress

e-mail info@oceanbooks.com.au
www.oceanbooks.com.au